Let what you love to eat inform the way you cook.

TETSUYA

Recipes from Australia's most acclaimed chef

# TETSUYA

TETSUYA WAKUDA

TEN SPEED PRESS
www.tenspeed.com

Copyright © 2001 by Tetsuya Wakuda
First published in 2000 by HarperCollins*Publishers,* Sydney, Australia

A Kirsty Melville Book

Ten Speed Press
PO Box 7123
Berkeley, California 94707
www.tenspeed.com

Distributed in Canada by Ten Speed Press Canada.

Library of Congress Cataloging-in-Publication Data

Wakuda, Tetsuya.
Tetsuya : recipes from Australia's most acclaimed chef / Tetsuya Wakuda.
p. cm.
Includes index.
ISBN 1-58008-294-7.
1. Cookery, Australian. 2. Cookery — Australia.
3. Wakuda, Tetsuya. I. Title.
TX725.A9 W35    2001
641.5994 — dc21        00-053527

Front cover recipe: roasting scampi seasoned with tea and scampi oil (see page 100)
Back cover recipe: confit of Petuna ocean trout with fennel salad (see pages 56, 59)
Body text written and recipes edited by Foong Ling Kong
Cover and internal design by Katie Mitchell
All internal recipe photographs by Takashi Morieda
Cover food photographs, black and white atmospheric and color kitchen photographs by Louise Lister
Cover and internal background photographs by David Lange

First printing, 2001
Printed in China through Phoenix Offset on 140gsm Kinmari Woodfree

1 2 3 4 5 6 7 8 9 10 — 05 04 03 02 01

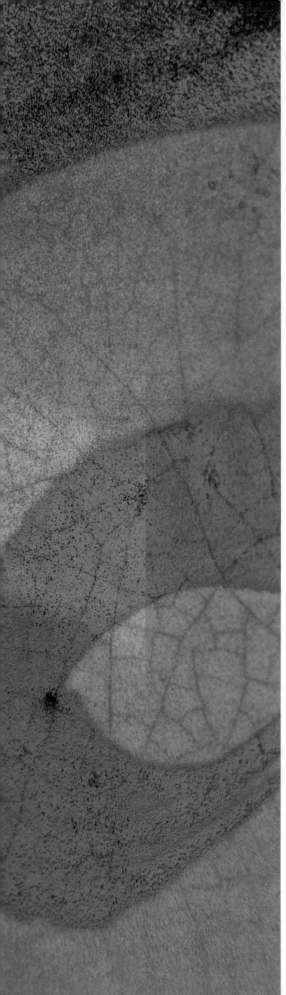

# Foreword

It is only once in a great while, perhaps every three or four years, that I meet someone with whom I form an instant and profound bond. Tetsuya Wakuda is one of those people. Although we live half a world apart, the force of his warm personality and amazing hospitality narrows the distance and time between us. After I tasted his cuisine it was evident to me that he absolutely loves to eat. Any chef who can prepare food that is so sensually satisfying has to have the same passion for eating. And, knowing Tetsuya the way I do, I can assure you that the love he has for eating thoroughly influences his culinary approach.

Before going on, I must relate how I first encountered Tetsuya. A few years ago I was cooking for a week in Melbourne. People kept saying to me, "Your culinary philosophy, your passion, your cuisine . . . remind me of chef Tetsuya. Are you planning to dine at his restaurant during your visit to Australia?" Unfortunately, I could not arrange to do so, as my one and only day in Sydney was being coordinated by the legendary Joan Campbell, and she (inexplicably!) had not made reservations at Tetsuya's. Moments after I arrived in my Sydney hotel room I received a phone call from a man I had never met who requested that I come and allow him to feed me at his restaurant – it was Tetsuya! I was stunned and felt like fate had intervened: we were destined to meet! Thirty minutes later I was at his restaurant. We greeted each other as though we were old friends and minutes later I was at the table. After an all-too-quick hour, and six sublime courses, I had to tear myself away to rendezvous with Ms. Campbell. Apparently omniscient, she knew exactly where I had been and chastised me for trying to squeeze in "another dinner," fearing I would be unable to eat at the restaurant she had selected. "Not a problem," I replied, and proceeded to eat the second meal (with a very big smile on my face, knowing I was already thoroughly fulfilled by meeting Tetsuya and tasting his creations). Since that day, my life has been touched by this amazing man and his utterly poetic cuisine.

Whenever I can, I find any excuse to cook with or, more importantly, to hang out with Tetsuya. I revel in his company. His peacefulness and calm have had an immensely positive effect on my approach to life and cooking. He is one of the few chefs I know whose way of being is completely in harmony with his cuisine. In both there is clarity, wholesomeness, and balance.

Tetsuya is part of an elite group of international chefs, along with Fredy Girardet, Alain Ducasse, Daniel Boulud, Ferran Adrià, and Thomas Keller, that has influenced other chefs through their personal styles and unique approaches to food. His culinary philosophy centers on pure, clean flavors that are decisive, yet completely refined. His amazing technique, Asian heritage, sincere humility, worldwide travels, and insatiable curiosity combine to create incredible, soulful dishes that exude passion in every bite.

This book is filled with a vast array of stunning creations, including many of his signature dishes, that are made approachable for the home cook. A typical example of a complex, yet accessible, dish is his confit of Petuna ocean trout with fennel salad (see pages 56, 59). It initially strikes the diner with clean, profound flavor, yet it is hauntingly delicate. The preparation allows each of the incredible products to speak for itself and combine in an intriguing juxtaposition.

One of the great joys of being a chef is dining out and sampling other styles of cuisine. I enjoy dining with food and wine connoisseurs and hearing their perspectives on different foods, but dining with Tetsuya is an altogether different experience. His passion for eating is as intense as his passion for cooking. Conversation is reserved for between courses. When there is interesting food in front of him, his entire focus remains on the dish. Surely the sensual and passionate way he eats greatly influences his aesthetic in the kitchen. For Tetsuya, I believe, the act of eating and cooking are one and the same. I love that. Even as I am writing this, I am contemplating staging a culinary event just to have an excuse to spend time with my great friend Tetsuya.

By the way, did I mention he loves to eat?

CHARLIE TROTTER

# Introduction

**As a child growing up** in Hamamatsu, a town in the prefecture of Shizuoka on Honshu in Japan, all foreign things fascinated me. I dreamed of living overseas, in lands where there were people with blond hair and blue eyes. The opportunity presented itself in 1982, when I was twenty-two. Armed with only one piece of information about the place – that there were lots of koalas and kangaroos around – and having only a limited grasp of English, I was deposited in the middle of Sydney by a cab driver. Sadly, there were no koalas and kangaroos, but I wasn't prepared to quibble too much. After all, I was *in* a Western country, where I could see *in real life* all the things I had only dreamed of!

**My very first job** was at Fishwives in Surry Hills. I still remember the thrill of my first small paycheck – riches that allowed me to indulge in one of my passions, hamburgers! To a newly arrived Japanese man, what could have epitomized Western food better?

**A year later** I was introduced to Sydney chef Tony Bilson, who was looking for a Japanese cook who could make sushi. Tony's kitchen at Kinsela's was where I realized I wanted to, and discovered that I could, cook. It was where I started learning classical French technique. I made up a lot of things along the way, and luckily for me, people liked the way it tasted.

I left Kinsela's in 1983, and, in partnership with the head waiter, opened Ultimo's. Sean Dwyer and I quickly learned about the responsibility of running our own business. I moved on and opened Tetsuya's Restaurant in Rozelle in 1989. This book is a celebration of the tenth anniversary of Tetsuya's.

**The journey has been exhilarating.** I am a very fortunate man: I have a job that allows me to do what I love, and to enjoy the good things in life.

But I am honest about my wants. I love to eat, and what I love to eat informs the way I cook. All the food has to be is *good*.

For me, good food comes about only if you put yourself in it. Food is for giving, and the act of cooking is a gift from the cook to the diner. The pleasure of the table comes from sharing, from the friend who says, "I want to cook for you." My appreciation is of their act of cooking.

As the host to those who sit at my table (and who read this book), I want all my guests and readers to feel welcome. The restaurant is my home, and when people walk in, they can have whatever they want. People come to restaurants for a treat, and when it's my treat, you can have what you like.

**Ingredients come first** with me. I love cooking seafood, and for me, there's nothing like going to the market and seeing what's fresh and wonderful for the day. The fresh market, the hawker center and the street food stalls are the places that sell and serve the food that real people eat and enjoy.

The produce we use in the restaurant kitchen is sourced from around Australia. It is a joy to work together with suppliers to search the country for the best possible produce.

**Make simplicity seem like abundance** – this is the lesson I take away from Japanese cuisine. I hope that diners will think that the food they eat in my restaurant is an honest use of prime produce, and appreciate the subtleties that I try to preserve. For me, a successful dish is when no one flavor overwhelms the other, but all coexist harmoniously.

There are no rules in food. You'll find French influences in my food. Some dishes have Chinese roots, and others Japanese. But the produce is all Australian.

**One dish leads to the other,** and builds on the taste and structure of the one before. The steamed before the broiled, the raw before the cooked.

The attention to the simple things in life – to the small things in life – is what I prize. Take the pageant of dishes that I serve at the restaurant, for instance. The *menu dégustation* is structured as a series of tiny tastes to highlight the entirety of the ingredients – their particular taste, texture, smell and look – whether they be from land, sea, or earth. In Japanese tradition, the greater the variety of food served, the greater the host's hospitality.

It is my hope that the food I cook at the restaurant satisfies many tastes.

**Don't be afraid of failure.** Even when it comes to my favorite, tried and tested recipes, I alter things all the time. Sometimes I shorten the cooking time; sometimes I cook for longer. I vary the temperature, add something or take something away. I may start off by poaching in oil instead of marinating, or poaching in stock instead of oil. I am flexible about everything, as long as the result is enjoyable.

Some of the dishes we cook at the restaurant have taken a long time to develop. For instance, the flourless chocolate cake took nearly eight months of experimentation till we came up with the cake we have today (see page 162). Temperatures for cooking the confit of ocean trout took three months of work until we got the color, the texture and the taste of the fish *exactly* right (see pages 56, 59). Cooking is an ongoing process, an endless game.

My cooking methods change all the time, depending on the season and the produce available. Cooking times also need constant adjustment according to the ingredient – is the ocean trout slightly thicker than usual today? Are the eggs very fresh?

We do not work from written recipes in the restaurant kitchen. The menus are often not designed until the last minute and, unfortunately for my team, dishes have been known to change midway during service just because a supplier has delivered a fresh ingredient!

**Learning is a discussion with others.** I have been inspired by a number of small, personal restaurants around the world. In Osaka, there exists a restaurant that seats eight people at a counter. The smallness of the restaurant is striking. I want to capture the essence of this restaurant – not because I aspire to turning away people who want to eat, but because of the attention the owner–chef lavishes on the little details.

**All I want** you to take away from this book is enjoyment.

## Notes on the recipes

The recipes in this book are not meant to be definitive, so please do not feel bound by them. I hope you use them as a source of ideas, and adjust the various elements to your taste.

Many of the ingredients I use may be a little hard to source outside of major cities or in places where you do not have access to Asian grocers, so please feel free to substitute ingredients as you see fit. If you are unsure of any ingredients, please refer to the glossary at the back of the book (see pages 171–173) for an explanation on what it is and where you can get it.

The size of servings in this book are not Western. We serve them in starter- or appetizer-sized portions in the restaurant. Please adjust the quantities upwards if you want to serve them as courses in their own right.

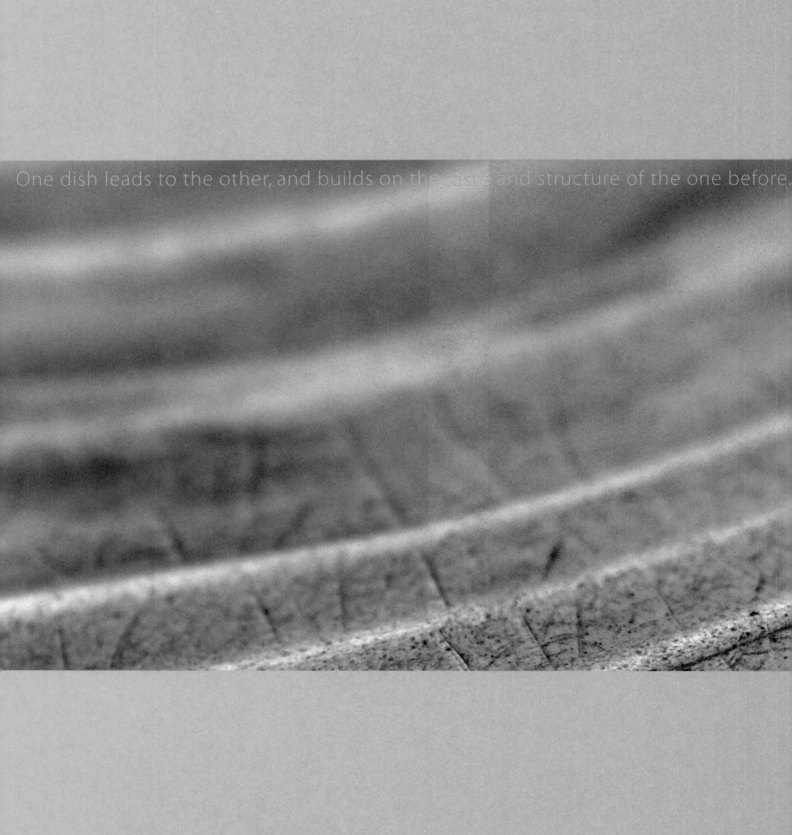
One dish leads to the other, and builds on the taste and structure of the one before.

The steamed before the broiled, the raw before the cooked.

## Consommé of Tomato and Tea

*For the best flavor, use very ripe tomatoes for this dish. Add a pinch of sugar to help the tomatoes along if they are lacking in flavor.*

4–5 medium-sized tomatoes, chopped
6 sundried tomatoes (not in oil)
600 ml (1 pint) water
½ teaspoon Ceylon tea
salt

Combine the tomatoes, sundried tomatoes, and water in a saucepan and cook over low heat until the flavors come together. Do not boil. Add the tea and allow to infuse over a very gentle heat.

Strain the liquid through muslin or an oil filter. Do not push on the remains – let the liquid drip through. Discard the solids.

Set the liquid aside for the sediment to settle. Before serving, skim off any scum, and pour off and discard the top liquid. Add a little salt to taste.

Pour into little bowls and serve immediately.

**SERVES 4**

*Wine suggestions*
Aromatic dry white: 2000 Meera Park Viognier; 1998 Calera "Harlan" Viognier; 1999 Yves Cuilleron Condrieu "Les Chaillots"

# Cold Soup of Cauliflower with Caviar

½ cauliflower
1 onion, finely chopped
1 tablespoon grapeseed oil
750 ml (1¼ pints) chicken stock
125 ml (4 fl oz) light cream or milk
salt and white pepper
1 drop light cream, lightly whipped
4 teaspoons caviar

Break the cauliflower into florets.

Sweat the onion in the oil. Do not allow to brown. Add the stock and cauliflower. Bring to a boil, reduce the heat to low, and cook about 5 minutes, or just until the cauliflower is tender.

Transfer the mixture to a bowl, and chill by placing the bowl on ice.

Blend the mixture in batches, adjusting the consistency with extra stock if necessary. Purée, and add the cream (or milk) until it reaches the desired consistency. Season to taste with salt and pepper.

Pour into bowls. Spoon a little whipped cream in the center and top with caviar.

**SERVES 4**

*Wine suggestions*
Medium to full-bodied chardonnay: 1998 Pierro Chardonnay; 1998 Forman Vineyards Chardonnay; Jean Pillot Chassagne-Montrachet "Caillerets"

## Cold Soup of Potato and Leek with Jellied Eggplant

1 eggplant (aubergine), peeled and julienned
300 ml (10 fl oz) chicken stock
1 tablespoon dashi (see page 169)
1 teaspoon mirin
2 teaspoons soy sauce
2 envelopes of gelatin
1 leek, chopped
1 onion, chopped
grapeseed oil
1 L (2 pints) chicken stock
6 potatoes, thinly sliced
200 ml (7 fl oz) milk
100 ml (3½ fl oz) light cream
salt and white pepper

GARNISH
chives, finely chopped
caviar

Keep the eggplant in water to stop discoloration and to draw out any bitterness. Squeeze out the water. Boil in the 10 fl oz stock with the dashi, mirin, and soy sauce until tender.

Soften the gelatin in some cold water, then add to the eggplant mixture, stirring until the gelatin dissolves. Refrigerate until set.

Sweat the leek and onion in some grapeseed oil. Add the 2 pints stock, then the potato. As soon as the potatoes are tender, cool down immediately. When ready to use, purée the mixture, adding milk and cream to reach the desired consistency. Taste for salt and pepper.

To serve, divide the eggplant between serving bowls, pour on the soup, and garnish with chives and caviar.

**SERVES 4**

*Wine suggestions*
Dry rosé: 2000 Charles Melton "Rose of Virginia"; 1998 Swanson Napa Valley Rosato; 1998 Château Rouet Rosé de Provence

## Cold Soup of Carrot and Saffron with Beancurd

1 large onion, finely chopped
1 small leek, finely chopped
6 medium-sized carrots, finely chopped
2 sticks celery, finely chopped
1.25 L (2 pints) chicken stock
1 pinch saffron threads
2 teaspoons soy sauce
salt and white pepper
125 ml (4 fl oz) soy milk
1 tablespoon beancurd
1 tablespoon soy milk
1 tablespoon finely chopped chives

Sweat the onion, leek, carrots, and celery in a small pan over low heat without any oil. Add the stock, saffron, and soy sauce, and cook until the vegetables are tender.

Purée the mixture, and add any leftover stock to achieve the desired consistency. Taste, and adjust the seasoning if necessary.

Cool, add the 4 oz soy milk, and check for seasoning again.

Purée the beancurd or push through a very fine sieve. Mix with the tablespoon soy milk. Place a little of the beancurd mixture in the center of the soup. Top with chives.

**SERVES 4**

*Wine suggestions*
Full-bodied rosé: 1999 Turkey Flat Rosé; 1998 Swanson Napa Valley Rosato; 1999 Domaine Tempier Bandol Rosé

## Cold Soup of Avocado with Caviar

*We serve this soup in small cups in the restaurant. You can increase the quantities to make a more substantial starter. If you are making ahead and keeping in the fridge, put some plastic wrap on the surface of the soup to prevent oxidization. Its consistency also changes once chilled.*

*Tonburi is a Japanese fern. If unavailable, use salmon roe caviar. Use Hass avocados if possible.*

1 avocado, peeled and sectioned
200–300 ml (7–10 fl oz) milk
salt and white pepper
1 pinch superfine sugar
2 tablespoons caviar or tonburi (mountain caviar)

The consistency of the soup changes depending on the speed of your blender, so start slowly and increase the speed until you get the consistency you like.

Purée the avocado and milk. Once it reaches the desired thickness, add salt and pepper to taste, and the sugar.

Pour into bowls, and serve topped with caviar or tonburi.

**SERVES 4**

*Wine suggestions*
Full-bodied sparkling wine or champagne: NV Domaine Chandon Brut 2000 Blanc de Noirs; Roederer Estate Brut L'Ermitage; NV Krug Grande Cuvée

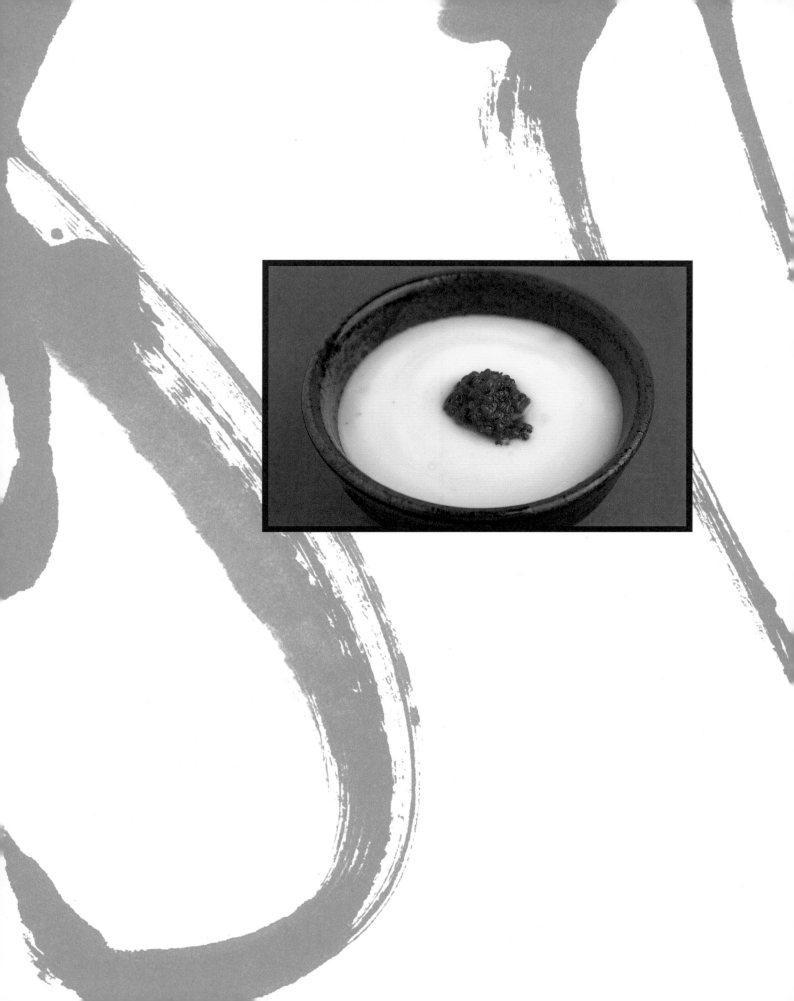

# Tasmanian Pacific Oysters with Rice Wine Vinaigrette

*The vinaigrette can be adapted for any number of oysters and can be made ahead of time and kept in the refrigerator.*

*Infuse 10 cm (4 in) konbu in a bottle of 750 ml (1¼ pints) rice wine vinegar for added flavor.*

ogonori (see page 169)
12 large Pacific oysters, shucked

VINAIGRETTE
1 teaspoon finely grated ginger
4 tablespoons rice wine vinegar
1 teaspoon superfine sugar
1 teaspoon soy sauce
6 tablespoons grapeseed oil
2 tablespoons olive oil
½ tablespoon lemon juice

GARNISH
chives, finely chopped
3 tablespoons ocean trout roe

To make the vinaigrette, whisk together all the ingredients in a bowl or jar.

Place a little ogonori on the base of the serving plate. Put the oysters on top and spoon over the vinaigrette.

Sprinkle the oysters with the chives and ocean trout roe.

**SERVES 4**

*Wine suggestions*
A good-quality Champagne or Méthode Champenoise: 1996 Taltarni "Clover Hill" Brut; 1995 Mumm Cuvée Napa; NV Louis Roederer Brut Premier

## Carpaccio of Snapper with Banyuls Dressing

*You can use any white-fleshed fish such as perch, flounder, bar cod, or whiting for this dish,
as long as it is of sashimi quality. White sesame oil is made from unroasted sesame seeds.
If you cannot find it, use grapeseed oil instead. Banyuls is a French-style vinegar
available from good food stores and delicatessens. If not available, use sherry
vinegar as a substitute.*

1 small cucumber, thinly sliced into rounds
100 g (3½ oz) snapper fillet, thinly sliced

VINAIGRETTE
2 tablespoons rice wine vinegar
1 tablespoon lemon juice
2 teaspoons Banyuls vinegar or sherry vinegar
salt and white pepper to taste
3–4 tablespoons white sesame oil
¼ teaspoon soy sauce

GARNISH
black sesame seeds
chives, cut into 2 cm (¾ in) lengths
mustard sprouts
baby shiso or mint leaves
sea salt

To make the vinaigrette, combine all the ingredients and mix well.

On a serving plate, arrange the cucumber rounds in a circle. Place
the snapper on top and spoon over some vinaigrette. Garnish with black sesame
seeds, chives, mustard sprouts, shiso and a few flakes of sea salt.

**SERVES 4**

*Wine suggestions*
Medium to full-bodied unoaked white: 1999 T'Gallant "Flag" Pinot Gris; 1998 Chalone Pinot
Blanc; 1998 Albert Mann Tokay Pinot Gris

## Chequerboard Tuna and Hamachi with Orange Oil

*A visually pleasing dish.*
*If you cannot find orange oil, infuse some grated zest in grapeseed oil.*

100 g (3½ oz) tuna
100 g (3½ oz) hamachi (kingfish)
¼ tablespoon ginger juice
¼ teaspoon orange oil
1 drop grapeseed oil
sea salt

If you like, trim the fish into square blocks. Cut the fish into 5 mm (¼ in) thick slices.

Combine the ginger juice, orange, and grapeseed oils and mix well.

Place the fish on serving plates in a checkerboard pattern and spoon over the vinaigrette. Place a few flakes of sea salt on top and serve.

**SERVES 4**

*Wine suggestions*
Aromatic, medium-bodied white: 1999 Henschke Gewürztraminer; 1998 Martinelli Gewürztraminer Martinelli Vineyard Select; 1998 Mann Gewürztraminer

# Marinated Whiting with Umeboshi

*The umeboshi (Japanese pickled plum) gives a freshness to the dish.*
*Adjust quantities to taste.*

150 g (5 oz) turbot fillet, skinned, boned, and julienned
1 pinch salt
1 tablespoon lemon juice
wakame (see page 170)

### VINAIGRETTE

2 teaspoons plum paste or 2 medium-sized umeboshi, ground to a paste
1 teaspoon soy sauce
1 teaspoon mirin
1 teaspoon light olive oil
salt and white pepper to taste

### GARNISH

chives, cut into 2.5 cm (1 in) lengths
4 small umeboshi, julienned
½ small green apple, julienned

To make the vinaigrette, combine all the ingredients and mix well.

Toss the fish with the vinaigrette, pinch of salt, and lemon juice.

To serve, place some wakame on the base of a serving plate. Place
the fish on top, and garnish with the chives, umeboshi, and apple.

**SERVES 4**

*Wine suggestions*
Medium-bodied chardonnay: 1997 Katnook Estate Chardonnay; 1998 Acacia
Chardonnay; 1997 Château de Fuissé Pouilly-Fuissé "Vielle Vignes"

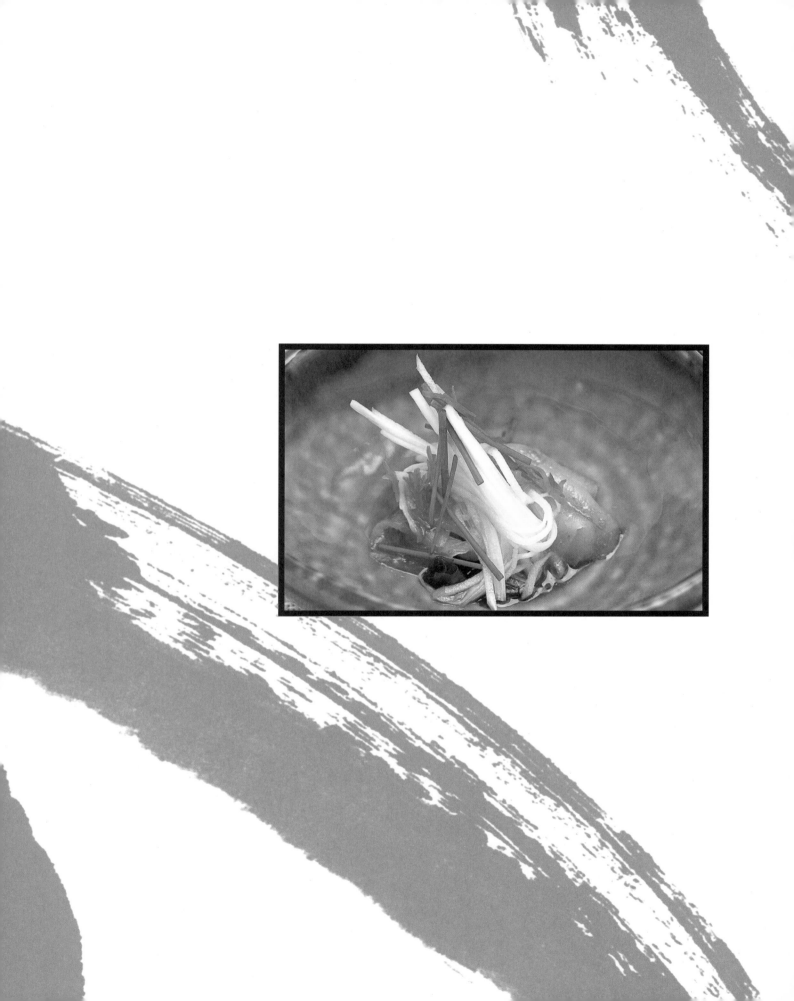

# Sea Scallops with Lemonade Fruit and Yuzu

*Lemonade fruit looks like a small lime, and its taste is refreshing and sensationally sweet.*
*If you can't find lemonade fruit, use lemon or lime juice instead, but add a little sugar.*

8 sea scallops

VINAIGRETTE
2 tablespoons lemonade fruit juice or lemon juice
2 tablespoons light olive oil
salt and pepper to taste

GARNISH
1 teaspoon finely chopped dried yuzu (use less if fresh)
2 lemonade fruit segments (if available)
chives, cut into 2 cm (¾ in) lengths
tarragon, finely chopped

Bring some water to a boil in a saucepan. Plunge the scallops into the boiling water, then remove immediately. The flesh should be just a little white. Place the scallops in some iced water to refresh, then pat dry.

To make the vinaigrette, combine all the ingredients. If using lemon juice, add a touch of superfine sugar.

Slice the scallops across thinly and place on the serving plate. Drizzle the vinaigrette on top, and garnish with yuzu, lemonade fruit segments, chives, and tarragon.

**SERVES 4**

*Wine suggestions*
Aromatic dry riesling: 2000 Jeffrey Grosset "Polish Hill" Riesling; 1998 Columbia Crest Johannisberg Riesling; 1998 Mann Riesling Grand Cru "Schlossberg"

## Celebrating ten years at Tetsuya's

Tetsuya's began as a little shopfront restaurant in the Sydney suburb of Rozelle, located in the city's west. It opened in 1989, to an Australia in the grip of an overheated economy, and on the threshold of a recession. That we survived to 1999 to celebrate ten years is a minor miracle.

How has the restaurant changed? The restaurant used to sit thirty-six people; today it seats fifty-five. We used to have an à la carte menu; today it's a *menu dégustation* (a tasting menu). As for our first kitchen, a reviewer once drolly commented that it was smaller than the inside of a stretch limo! The kitchen is still small, and precludes us from doing certain things, but it's a luxury compared to what we started with. The kitchen team has also expanded considerably – from a one-man show with the help of a kitchenhand, we now have a team of twelve in the kitchen, and ten service staff.

It's embarrassing to recount now, but the early visitors had it hard. They put up with a disorganized restaurant and erratic service. I am grateful they persevered with us, and allowed us to learn through trial and error. For example, the restaurant used to have doors that, in winter, opened to let out all the heat in the restaurant – people kept their coats on during the meal. Finally, we were compelled to move the doors. The bathrooms were located outside, at the back of the restaurant, and on rainy nights, the best we could do was offer napkins for patrons to dry themselves when they came back in.

The food today is more labor-intensive. Where we once had a hand-written menu, there is none now. Dishes arrive course by course at a leisurely pace, and sometimes diners ask for a list of courses when they leave. And look at the dishes from when we started – "boudin of pork and duck liver and pig's trotters with port wine and mustard sauce," "grilled breast of duck with duck sausage, sage and orange and ginger" and "warm salad of fried marinated quail with rice and lemon vinaigrette" – quite different from what we serve today, although I can see in that menu the beginnings of what we now have on the *menu dégustation*.

I take my inspiration from all over, be it from a trip back home to Japan, or to Italy, or other parts of Asia or the Mediterranean. Dishes may seem to remain for a long time, and the descriptions certainly stay the same, but they would have changed subtly and slowly in their spicing, cooking technique, and mood. Even our signature dishes are not immune to tinkering and refining. To me, nothing is ever so perfect that it cannot be improved.

We simply prepare food that takes my fancy, which may be from an ingredient that captures my imagination that minute, that day, that week, that month. It's an intensely personal perspective, and I am grateful that many people enjoy it.

As well as the food being "just right," the aesthetics of the actual restaurant are also important to me. The dining experience should be one of visual as well as gastronomic pleasure. An important contribution to the artworks displayed in the restaurant was made by my good friend Akio Makigawa before he passed away on Christmas Eve, 1999. When he gave me his symbolic sculptures, Akio said, "This is the water and the seed. I want you to grow." I am proud to display his works in my restaurant and look on them as an inspiration as well as a fond reminder of my dear friend.

So the restaurant has been fortunate to make it past its tenth birthday, and, in that time, to have found a form. For that, I have to thank our loyal clientele, who have stuck with us through the years and helped us to grow the way Akio would have wanted.

## Marinated Trevally with Preserved Lemon

*Taste this dish as you are making it – you may need to adjust the lemon and salt quantities,
depending on the strength of the preserved lemons. It makes a lovely starter and canapé.*

200 g (7 oz) yellowtail fillet, skinned, trimmed and julienned
1 teaspoon very finely chopped preserved lemon, or to taste
½ tablespoon finely chopped chives
½ tablespoon finely chopped parsley
reduced-salt soy sauce (optional)
white pepper
1 teaspoon mirin
½ teaspoon finely grated ginger
2 teaspoons white sesame oil or grapeseed oil

GARNISH
chives
baby shiso or mint leaves

Mix all the ingredients together, and adjust the seasoning to taste.
If you can't find preserved lemon, use lemon zest or lime, adjusting
the salt content with soy sauce to taste.

Place on serving plates, and garnish with chives and shiso.

**SERVES 4**

*Wine suggestions*
Full-bodied chardonnay: 1998 Dromana Estate Reserve Chardonnay;
1997 Vincent et Francois Jouard Chassagne-Montrachet "Morgeot";
1997 Flowers Chardonnay

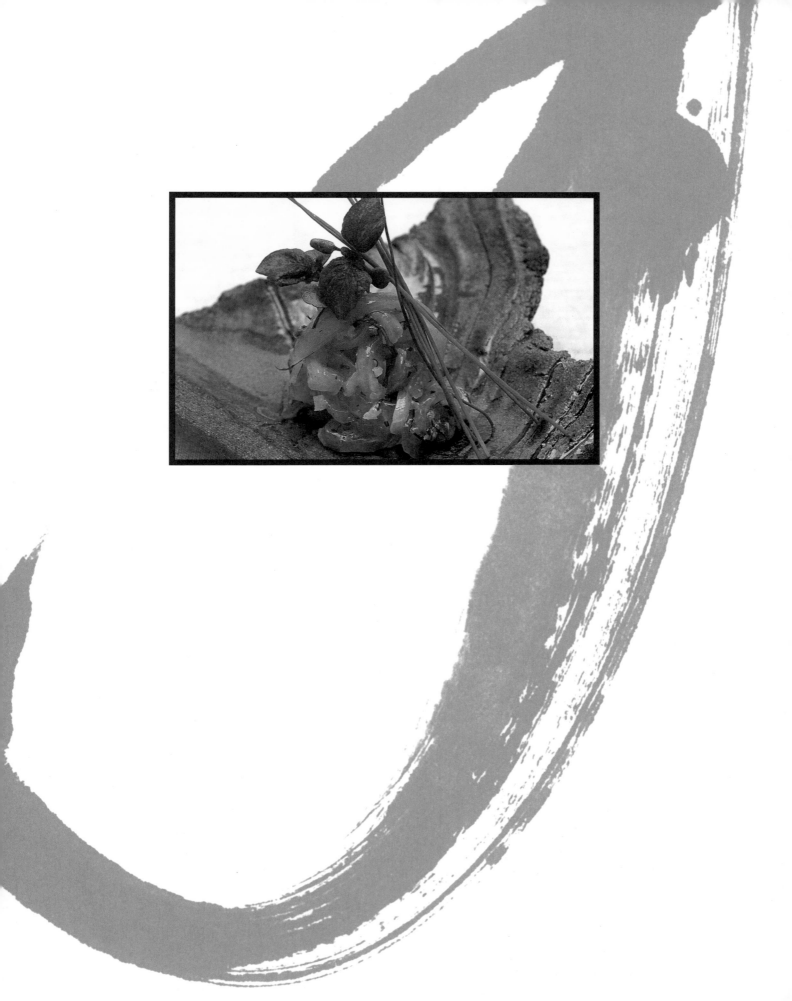

## Seared Tuna with Apple and Olive

200 g (7 oz) tuna fillet, trimmed into a square block
grapeseed oil
1 tablespoon finely grated green apple
1 tablespoon finely grated daikon
1 teaspoon white sesame oil
salt and pepper to taste
½ teaspoon lemon juice
bamboo leaf
½ tablespoon soy sauce
½ tablespoon mirin

GARNISH
⅓ teaspoon black olive paste
shiso or mint leaf, julienned
black sesame seeds

In a non-stick pan, sear the tuna in a little grapeseed oil over a very low heat until the flesh just turns white. Cool and slice thinly into 5 mm (¼ in) pieces.

Combine the grated apple and daikon with the white sesame oil, salt, pepper and lemon juice.

Place the bamboo leaf on a serving plate. Place the tuna on top. Mix the soy sauce and mirin together and spoon over the tuna. Spoon on a little green apple and daikon mixture. Garnish with a little of the olive paste, shiso, and black sesame seeds.

**SERVES 4**

*Wine suggestions*
Full-bodied roussanne: 1998 St Huberts Roussanne; 1998 Cline Cellars Roussanne Los Carneros; 1998 Yves Cuilleron St Joseph "Le Coteau St Pierre" Roussanne

# Sashimi of Hamachi with Blood Orange and Ginger Vinaigrette

*Grapefruit can be used in place of the blood orange.*

120 g (4 oz) hamachi (kingfish), thinly sliced
1 blood orange, segmented and all pith removed

GINGER VINAIGRETTE
1 drop orange oil
1 drop Banyuls vinegar or sherry vinegar
¼ teaspoon finely grated ginger
1 teaspoon soy sauce
¼ teaspoon finely crushed garlic
salt and black pepper to taste

GARNISH
chives, finely chopped
baby cilantro leaves
green onions (scallions), thinly sliced
parsley, finely julienned
baby mâche or baby spinach leaves

For the vinaigrette, combine all the ingredients and mix well.

Arrange the fish on a plate. Add the blood orange, then drizzle over the vinaigrette.

Garnish with chives, cilantro, green onions, parsley, and mâche.

**SERVES 4**

*Wine suggestions*
Aromatic dry white: 1999 Barrington Estates Gewürztraminer; 1998 Kendall Jackson Gewürztraminer Vintners Reserve; 1998 Hugel Gewürztraminer

# Tian of Marinated Scampi with Pawpaw, Cucumber and Tonburi

2 small scampi, halved
¼ teaspoon walnut oil
1 teaspoon grapeseed oil
1 drop Banyuls vinegar or sherry vinegar
½ teaspoon finely chopped chives
1 pinch salt
1 pinch white pepper
¼ teaspoon lemon or lime juice
4 tablespoons finely diced papaya
4 tablespoons finely diced cucumber
4 heaped teaspoons tonburi (mountain caviar) or standard caviar

Take the meat out of the scampi and finely dice. Mix the scampi with the walnut oil, grapeseed oil, vinegar, chives, salt, white pepper, and lemon juice.

Put a ring mold of 5 cm (2 in) diameter on each serving plate. Fill, first with a layer of papaya, followed by a layer of cucumber, scampi, and caviar. Remove the ring and serve.

**SERVES 4**

*Wine suggestions*
Aromatic dry white: 2000 Heggies Viognier; 1998 Joseph Phelps Viognier; 1998 René Rostaing Condrieu "La Bonette"

# Salad of Sea Scallops with Asparagus and Beans

4 sea scallops
8 butter beans, sliced diagonally
8 green beans, julienned
4 asparagus, sliced diagonally
1 tablespoon peeled and diced tomato
1 pinch julienned leek
chives, cut into 2 cm (¾ in) lengths
¼ teaspoon finely chopped tarragon
1 pinch salt
1 pinch white pepper
a dash of lemon juice
1 drop light olive oil
baby mâche or baby spinach leaves

VINAIGRETTE
1 tablespoon white sesame seed paste
1 teaspoon soy sauce
1 teaspoon mirin
1 tablespoon grapeseed oil
¼ teaspoon minced garlic

In a hot non-stick frying pan with no oil, sear the scallops until the surface is a light brown color. Rest and chill, then thinly slice across.

To make the vinaigrette, combine all the ingredients and mix well.

Toss together the scallops, beans, asparagus, tomato, leek, chives, tarragon, salt, pepper, lemon juice, and olive oil.

Divide the salad between 4 serving plates and pour the vinaigrette over. Garnish with some baby mâche.

**SERVES 4**

*Wine suggestions*
Dry white semillon or sauvignon blanc blend: 1998 Whitehall Lane Sauvignon Blanc; 2000 Brokenwood Semillon; 1998 Pascal Jolivet Sancerre

## Tian of Smoked Ocean Trout with Truffle and Olives

160 g (5½ oz) lightly smoked ocean trout, finely diced
½ teaspoon black olive paste
2 teaspoons black truffle paste
½ tablespoon finely julienned parsley
1 pinch salt
1 pinch black pepper
½ tablespoon finely chopped chives
1 drop lemon-scented oil
2 teaspoons goat cheese or goat curd
4 arugula leaves
baby mâche or baby spinach leaves

Mix the ocean trout with the black olive paste, black truffle paste, parsley, salt, black pepper, and chives.

In a separate bowl, mix the lemon-scented oil with the goat cheese to soften.

To serve, place a little goat cheese on the plate. Put a rocket leaf on top, then sit a small ring mold on it. Fill the mold with the ocean trout mixture. Remove the mold, and garnish with baby mâche or baby spinach leaves.

**SERVES 4**

*Wine suggestions*
Medium-bodied chardonnay: 1998 Nepenthe Chardonnay; 1997 Staglin Family Vineyard Chardonnay; 1997 Guy Roulot Meursault "Les Suchets"

# Tartare of Marinated Scampi with Tomato and Pepper Sorbet

flesh from 6 small scampi, finely chopped
$\frac{1}{2}$ teaspoon finely chopped chives
1 pinch celery salt
$\frac{1}{4}$ teaspoon walnut oil
1 drop Banyuls vinegar or sherry vinegar

TOMATO AND PEPPER SORBET
6 medium-sized very ripe tomatoes
200 ml (7 fl oz) tomato juice
salt and white pepper
1 pinch superfine sugar
1 tablespoon lemon juice

GARNISH
4 teaspoons peeled and diced tomato
4 sprigs chervil
lemon-scented oil

To make the sorbet, purée the tomatoes, skin, seeds, and all, in a blender. Add the tomato juice, salt and pepper to taste, sugar, and lemon juice. Transfer the mixture to an ice-cream machine and churn according to the manufacturer's instructions.

Mix the scampi with the chives, celery salt, walnut oil, and vinegar.

To serve, put a small ring mold on the base of a serving plate. Place a little scampi in the base of the mold. Remove the mold. Garnish with the diced tomato and chervil. Top with a small scoop of sorbet. Put a small drop of lemon-scented oil on the sorbet. Repeat with the rest of the ingredients.

**SERVES 4**

*Wine suggestions*
Medium-bodied chardonnay: 1998 Howard Park Chardonnay; 1998 Patz and Hall Wine Co. Chardonnay Napa; 1997 Jean Dauvissat Chablis "Montmains"

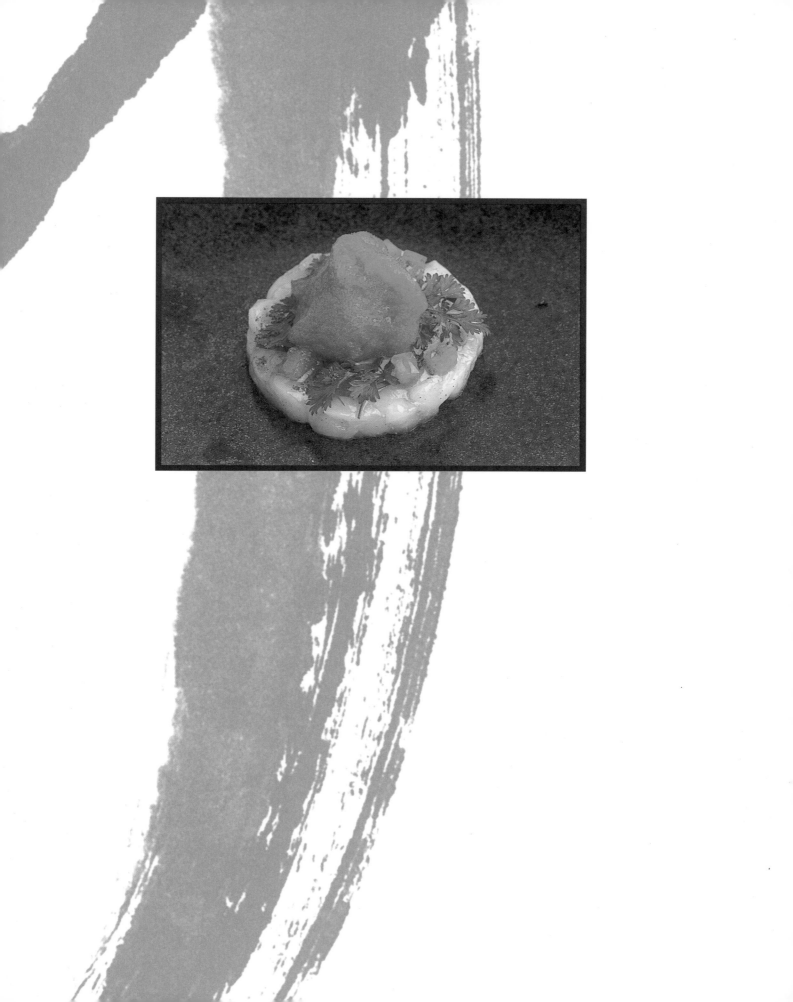

## Tartare of Ocean Trout with Sushi Rice, Avocado, and Grapes

*Ocean trout is called steelhead trout in America.*

4 tablespoons finely diced ocean trout
2 tablespoons steamed sushi rice
2 tablespoons diced avocado
½ tablespoon finely chopped parsley
20 green grapes, peeled, quartered, and seeded
grated zest of ½ lemon
2 tablespoons ocean trout roe
2 tablespoons wasabi mayonnaise (see page 170)
4 sprigs chervil

In a bowl, mix together the ocean trout, rice, avocado, parsley, grapes, and lemon zest. Add the ocean trout roe and wasabi mayonnaise.

Divide between 4 serving plates and garnish each with a sprig of chervil.

**SERVES 4**

*Wine suggestions*
Aromatic dry white: 1998 Coriole Chenin Blanc; 1998 Pine Ridge Chenin Blanc/Viognier; 1998 Domaine de la Aubuisières Vouvray Sec "Silex"

## Cuttlefish Noodles with Quail Egg

2 medium-sized squid
1 teaspoon chopped chives
$\frac{1}{4}$ teaspoon lemonade fruit zest
$\frac{1}{2}$ teaspoon finely chopped salted capers
1 teaspoon grapeseed oil
$1\frac{1}{2}$ teaspoons mirin
$1\frac{1}{2}$ teaspoons soy sauce
4 very small broccoli florets, blanched
4 quail egg yolks

GARNISH
aonori
1 pinch julienned lemon zest

Clean the squid and peel off the skin. Score the squid hoods, then slice along the length of the hoods into very thin strips that resemble noodles.

Toss the squid with the chives, lemonade fruit zest, capers, oil, mirin, soy sauce, and broccoli.

Form the squid into mounds in 4 serving bowls, making a little well in the center of each. Slide a quail yolk onto each well.

Garnish with a sprinkling of aonori and lemon zest before serving.

**SERVES 4**

*Wine suggestions*
Full-bodied chardonnay: 1998 Dalwhinnie Chardonnay; 1997 Au Bon Climat "Le Bouge" Chardonnay; 1997 Jean Boillot et Fils Meursault "Genevrieres"

# Tartare of Tuna with Goat's Cheese

*Make sure the cheese is not too salty.*

250 g (8 oz) tuna, finely diced
1 pinch white pepper
1 tablespoon olive oil
1 teaspoon finely chopped anchovies
60 g (2 oz) fresh goat cheese, finely chopped
¾ tablespoon finely chopped chives
½ tablespoon soy sauce
½ tablespoon mirin
1 pinch sea salt
1 pinch cayenne pepper
1 pinch finely chopped garlic
½ teaspoon finely chopped ginger

GARNISH
baby shiso or mint
mâche or baby spinach leaves

Mix together all the ingredients.

Divide between 4 serving plates, and garnish with shiso and mâche leaves.

**SERVES 4**

*Wine suggestions*
Ripe-style sauvignon blanc: 1999 Taltarni Sauvignon Blanc; 1998 Ironhouse Sauvignon Blanc; 1998 Vacheron Sancerre

# The story of a fish

The ocean trout was first a salmon.

Our signature dish of confit of Petuna ocean trout with fennel salad is nearly eight years old, and started its life as a salmon dish. When the salmon was between seasons, my suppliers, Peter and Una Rockcliff at Petuna, would offer me ocean trout to bridge the gap. I ended up liking the complex, rich taste of the ocean trout more than that of the salmon, and used it to replace the latter.

In those days, the quality of the fish varied a little; most days they were good, but on some they were exceptional. On one of those exceptional days, I hopped on the phone to the suppliers to see what they were doing to produce fish of such quality. Since then we have worked together to get the fish to a consistent quality, and fixed the conditions so that we can maintain the size, color, fat content, and taste.

The story of the fish is an interesting one. The fish are raised in fresh water and, after a year, moved to Macquarie Harbour in Tasmania, where the waters are brackish and the currents strong. Being brackish, the water is dark and the fish runs little risk of sunburn. The waters also mean the fish remains free of gill disease. We take the fish when it is 7 to 8 pounds in weight.

Over the years, the ocean trout has undergone every cooking technique you can imagine: it has been poached, grilled, and today, it is gently cooked in Spanish or Italian olive oil. The accompaniments have included marinated red bell pepper, celery, fennel, and salmon roe. The one constant is the kelp, a favorite ingredient I like to use in place of salt.

I have domesticated the recipe from the way we cook it at the restaurant to ensure that it will work and taste the same for you in the home. I cooked it in this manner when I was cooking with my friend Charlie Trotter in New York.

If you cannot find ocean trout use steelhead trout in its place.

# Confit of Petuna Ocean Trout with Fennel Salad

*Ocean trout is known as steelhead trout in America.*

350 g (11 oz) ocean trout, filleted
100 ml (3 ½ fl oz) grapeseed oil
80 ml (2 ½ fl oz) olive oil
½ tablespoon ground coriander
½ teaspoon white pepper
10 whole leaves basil
3 sprigs thyme
¼ teaspoon finely chopped garlic
2 stalks celery, finely chopped
2 small carrots, finely chopped
3 tablespoons chopped chives
4 tablespoons konbu, finely chopped
½ teaspoon sea salt
2 tablespoons ocean trout caviar

PARSLEY OIL
leaves from ¼ bunch Italian parsley
100 ml (3 ½ fl oz) olive oil or grapeseed oil
½ tablespoon salted capers, rinsed and drained

FENNEL SALAD
¼ bulb fennel, shaved
1 teaspoon lemon juice
salt and pepper
½ teaspoon lemon-scented oil

Skin the ocean trout and cut crosswise into 70–80 g (2 ½ oz) pieces – they should weigh no more than 100 g (3 ½ oz). In a little tray, immerse the ocean trout in grapeseed oil and olive oil with the coriander, pepper, basil, thyme, and garlic. Cover and allow to marinate for a few hours in the fridge. If you do not want to use too much oil, paint the surface of the fish with oil and press on the herbs.

To cook the fish, first preheat the oven to the absolutely lowest setting possible.

Take the fish out of the oil and allow to come to room temperature. Chop the celery and carrots and place on the base of a baking tray. Put the ocean trout on top and place in the oven. Cook with the door open so that the fish cooks gently. Paint the surface every few minutes with the marinade.

*continued page 59*

Depending on the size and thickness of the fish, cooking takes 7–8 minutes (no more than 10 minutes). When you touch the end part, your finger should just go through the flesh. The flesh should not have changed color at all, but remain a brilliant orangey-red, and feel lukewam to the touch.

Remove the fish from the oven and allow to cool down immediately. Lift out of the tray and allow to come to room temperature.

To make the parsley oil, purée the parsley with the olive oil in a blender. Add the capers and blend.

To make the fennel salad, thinly slice the fennel on a mandolin. Toss with the lemon juice, salt and pepper to taste, and some lemon-scented oil or lemon zest.

Sprinkle the top of the fish with finely chopped chives, konbu, and a little sea salt.

To serve, place some fennel salad on the base of the plate. Put the ocean trout on top and drizzle a little parsley oil all around. Dot the ocean trout caviar at regular intervals, and serve.

**SERVES 4**

*Wine suggestions*

A complex chardonnay: 1997 Leeuwin Estate Art Series; 1997 Kistler Chardonnay "Durrel"; or a 1997 Jean Boillot et Fils Puligny Montrachet "Clos de la Mouchere"

## Salad of Tataki Bonito with Garlic Chips and Shiso

2 x 150 g (5 oz) bonito fillets, skin on (or any other tuna)
1 teaspoon brandy (optional)
sea salt
1 tablespoon olive oil
4 large iceberg lettuce leaves, thinly sliced
2 tablespoons finely chopped green onions (scallions)
8 shiso or mint leaves, chopped
4 tablespoons enoki mushrooms, washed in water and a little lemon juice, drained
1 tablespoon julienned nori

MARINADE
100 ml (3½ fl oz) rice vinegar
100 ml (3½ fl oz) light soy sauce
2 tablespoons sake
3 tablespoons mirin
10 g (⅓ oz) dried bonito flakes
2 tablespoons lemon juice
1 teaspoon grated ginger
½ teaspoon chopped garlic

GARLIC CHIPS AND OIL
300 ml (10 fl oz) olive oil
8 cloves garlic, peeled and thinly sliced

To make the marinade, combine the rice vinegar, soy sauce, sake, mirin, bonito flakes, and lemon juice in a saucepan and bring to a boil. Remove from the heat and cool.

Place the bonito fillets skin side down on the counter and cut along each side of the bones in the middle of the fillet, leaving 4 half-fillets. Brush the bonito with brandy, if using, sprinkle with sea salt, cover, and refrigerate for at least 30 minutes, or up to 5 hours.

Heat the olive oil in a frying pan and quickly sear the bonito, skin side first, over a very high heat, or sear with a blowtorch. Place the bonito on ice to stop the cooking process and cool. Pat dry with a paper towel.

Add the ginger and garlic to the cooled, strained marinade and taste. If it's too salty, add a little cold water. Place bonito, skin side down, in a shallow roasting pan and pour over enough marinade to cover. Cover and refrigerate for 2 hours.

*continued page 62*

To make the garlic chips, heat the olive oil over very low heat, add the garlic, and continue to cook over low heat for about 15 minutes until the garlic is crisp but not brown, and the oil is well flavored. Remove the chips with a slotted spoon, drain on paper towels, and reserve the oil.

To serve, remove bonito from the marinade and pat dry with absorbent paper. Cut into 5 mm (⅛ in) thick slices and fan out on 4 serving plates. Pile lettuce into the center and sprinkle green onions and shiso over the fish. Top with enoki mushrooms and nori, sprinkle with a few garlic chips, and drizzle with a little of the garlic oil and a little of the marinade.

**SERVES 4**

*Wine suggestions*
Dry semillon/sauvignon blend: 1999 Cullens Reserve Semillon Sauvignon Blanc; 1998 Merryvale Sauvignon Blanc Reserve; 1998 Pavillon Blanc de Margaux

# Tataki of Loin of Venison with Rosemary and Honey Vinaigrette

200 g (7 oz) venison loin, thinly sliced

VINAIGRETTE
100 ml (3½ fl oz) grapeseed oil
2 tablespoons white wine vinegar
2 tablespoons honey
1 teaspoon soy sauce
1 teaspoon finely chopped rosemary
1 pinch salt
1 pinch white pepper

GARNISH
freshly ground black pepper
chives, finely chopped
white truffle oil (optional)

To make the vinaigrette, combine all the ingredients and mix well.

Arrange the sliced venison on a serving plate and drizzle the vinaigrette all around. Garnish with black pepper, chives, and white truffle oil.

**SERVES 4**

*Wine suggestions*
Medium to full-bodied shiraz: 1998 Frankland Estate "Isolation" Shiraz; 1997 Jade Mountain Syrah; 1998 Domaine Courbis St-Joseph

# Tataki of Ostrich with Truffled Peaches

200 g (7 oz) ostrich (fan fillet), thinly sliced

SAUCE
2 tablespoons soy sauce
2 tablespoons mirin
1 pinch ground sansho
$\frac{1}{2}$ teaspoon finely chopped garlic
$\frac{1}{2}$ teaspoon grated ginger
1 teaspoon superfine sugar

GARNISH
2 truffled wild peaches, thinly sliced
chives, cut into 2 cm ($\frac{3}{4}$ in) lengths
4 sprigs watercress

To make the sauce, combine all the ingredients and mix well.

Divide the sliced ostrich between 4 serving plates. Spoon over a little sauce, and garnish with the peaches, chives, and watercress.

**SERVES 4**

*Wine suggestions*
Medium to full-bodied pinot noir: 1998 Coldstream Hills Reserve Pinot Noir; 1997 David Bruce Pinot Noir Central Coast; 1997 Hubert Lignier Morey St Denis "Chaffots"

## Salad of Blood Orange, Beetroot and Rhubarb

2 medium-sized beets
1 stalk rhubarb, thinly sliced diagonally
1 teaspoon superfine sugar
1 pinch salt
2 blood oranges
4 sprigs chervil

### VINAIGRETTE
½ teaspoon walnut oil
1 teaspoon Banyuls vinegar or sherry vinegar
1 pinch salt
1 pinch white pepper

Preheat the oven to 200°C (400°F).

Wrap the beets in foil and roast in the oven for 20–30 minutes, or until tender. Allow to come to room temperature, then peel. Cut each beet into 10–12 segments.

Toss the rhubarb with the sugar and salt.

Segment the oranges, and remove all the pith.

To make the vinaigrette, combine all the ingredients in a small bowl.

Place the cut beets in a mixing bowl. Add the rhubarb, blood orange, and the vinaigrette. Mix to distribute the flavors.

Divide the salad between 4 plates. Garnish with a sprig of chervil.

**SERVES 4**

*Wine suggestions*
Aromatic dry white: 1999 Clonakilla Viognier; 1998 Alban Vineyards Viognier; 1999 Robert Niero Condrieu

## Seasonal Garden Greens with Soy and Balsamic Vinaigrette

80 g (2½ oz) mixed salad greens

VINAIGRETTE
80 ml (2½ fl oz) grapeseed oil
80 ml (2½ fl oz) olive oil
1 tablespoon soy sauce
3 tablespoons mirin
2 tablespoons balsamic vinegar
½ teaspoon finely minced garlic

To make the vinaigrette, combine all the ingredients and mix well.

Place the mixed leaves in a bowl and toss with the vinaigrette until well coated.

**SERVES 4**

*Wine suggestions*
Dry semillon or semillon/sauvignon blend: 1999 Glenguin Semillon;
1998 Brander Vineyard Sauvignon Blanc; 1997 Château Clos Floridene

# Lobster Ravioli with Tomato and Basil Vinaigrette

200 g (7 oz) raw lobster meat or prawns, finely chopped and chilled
200 g (7 oz) sea scallops, peeled and chilled
½ teaspoon finely chopped tarragon
1 tablespoon finely chopped chives
300 ml (10 fl oz) light cream, chilled
salt and black pepper
1 egg white, lightly beaten
24 wonton wrappers
wakame (see page 170)

### TOMATO AND BASIL VINAIGRETTE
100 ml (3½ fl oz) extra virgin olive oil
1½ tablespoons rice wine vinegar (infused with konbu)
½ cup peeled and diced tomato
1 teaspoon ground coriander
½ teaspoon finely chopped basil
¼ teaspoon finely chopped garlic
salt and white pepper, to taste
1 pinch superfine sugar

### GARNISH
flying fish roe
finely julienned basil

Make sure all the ingredients and the bowl of the food processor are well chilled before you start.

Purée the lobster and scallops in a food processor. Once they are finely blended, add the tarragon, chives, and 100 ml (3½ fl oz) of the cream and blend again quickly. Do not over-blend or the cream will separate. Fold in the rest of the cream by hand, add salt and pepper to taste.

Paint some egg white onto a wonton wrapper. Put a spoonful of the lobster mixture on top, and place another wonton wrapper on top. Press the edges to seal, then cut into rounds with a pastry cutter. Repeat with the rest of the wonton wrappers and filling. Set aside until ready to cook.

To make the vinaigrette, combine all the ingredients and mix well.

Bring lots of salted water to a boil. Drop the ravioli into the boiling water and cook until they float to the surface.

Place some wakame on the base of 4 serving bowls. Place the ravioli on top, and drizzle over the vinaigrette. Garnish with flying fish roe and basil.

**SERVES 4**

*Wine suggestions*
Full-bodied chardonnay: 1998 Giaconda Chardonnay; 1998 Palmeyer Chardonnay; 1997 Yves Boyer Martenot Meursault "Genevriers"

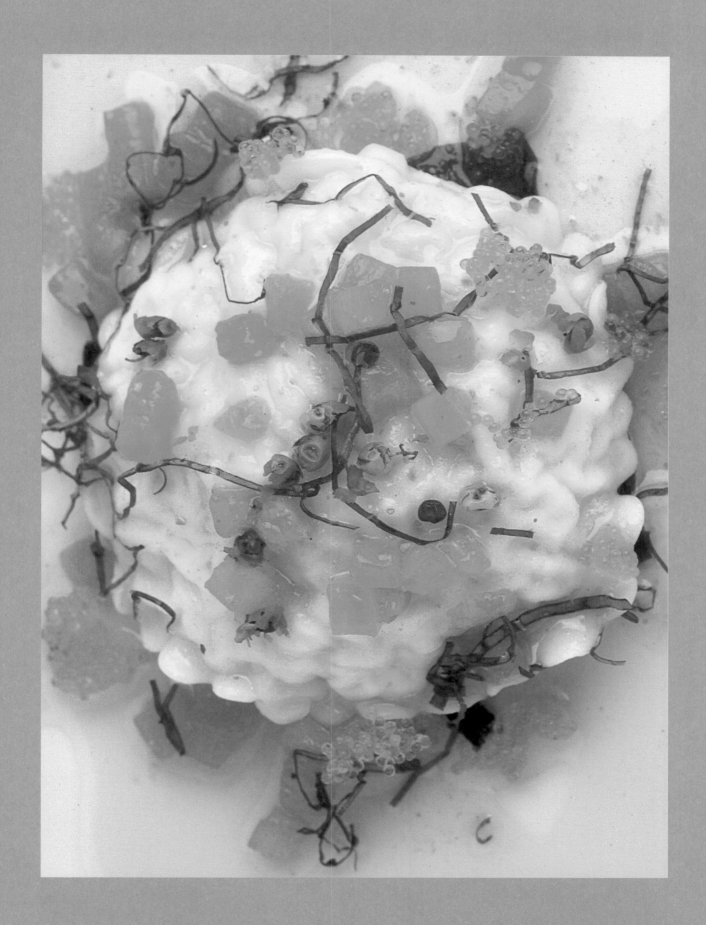

## Angel Hair Pasta with Scampi and Scampi Oil

*A light but rich dish, ideal as an entrée. You might need to increase the quantity of the scampi oil used, so taste as you go. Watch the quantity of garlic – the finished dish shouldn't really taste of it, so use just a touch to lift the flavor. You can use prawns in place of the scampi.*

150 g (5 oz) angel hair pasta
3 tablespoons scampi oil (see pages 169–170)
4 scampi or medium-sized prawns, cut into small pieces
¼ teaspoon finely chopped tarragon
1 pinch salt
1 pinch white pepper
½ tablespoon chopped chives
1 teaspoon soy sauce
1 teaspoon mirin
1 small pinch finely chopped garlic

Place the angel hair pasta in a large saucepan of boiling water. Cook for 2–3 minutes, or until al dente. Rinse the pasta in cold water, drain well, and set aside.

Combine the scampi oil, scampi, tarragon, salt, pepper, chives, soy sauce, mirin, and garlic in a frying pan and put on the heat. Once the scampi meat starts to change color, add the drained pasta. Toss well to combine, adjust the seasoning if necessary, and serve.

**SERVES 4**

*Wine suggestions*
Medium-bodied chardonnay: 1998 Green Vineyard Chardonnay; 1998 Quipe Chardonnay Bien Nacido Vineyard; 1999 Domaine Collonges Pouilly-Fuissé

## Cold Spaghettini with Cauliflower and Sea Urchin Roe

1 recipe cauliflower soup (see page 12)
1 hard-boiled egg
100 g (3½ oz) spaghettini
1 tablespoon sea urchin roe
2 teaspoons finely chopped chives
4 teaspoons caviar
mâche or baby spinach leaves

Prepare the cauliflower soup according to the instructions on page 12.

Grate the hard-boiled egg through a fine sieve to get a light powder. Cook the spaghettini in lots of boiling salted water until soft – not al dente.

To serve, toss the pasta with the cauliflower soup, grated egg, sea urchin roe, chives, and caviar.

Divide into serving plates and garnish with mâche.

**SERVES 4**

*Wine suggestions*
Full-bodied chardonnay: 1998 Landmark Vineyards Chardonnay Overlook; 1997 Mount Adam Chardonnay; 1999 Thevenet "Domaine Bongrans" Mâcon Clesse

## Angel Hair Pasta with Asparagus and Truffle Oil

250 g (8 oz) angel hair pasta
2 tablespoons grapeseed oil
1 pinch salt
1 pinch white pepper
1 tablespoon finely chopped shallots
1 bunch asparagus, trimmed and sliced diagonally
100 ml (3 1/2 fl oz) chicken stock
2 teaspoons mirin
1 teaspoon soy sauce
1/2 clove garlic, finely chopped
1 pinch superfine sugar
1 teaspoon finely chopped parsley
1 teaspoon finely chopped basil
1 tablespoon finely chopped chives
1 teaspoon truffle oil

Place the angel hair pasta in a large saucepan of boiling water. Cook for 2–3 minutes, or until al dente. Rinse the pasta in cold water, drain well, and set aside.

Heat the grapeseed oil in a frying pan over medium to high heat, add salt and pepper, the shallots and asparagus, and sauté until tender.

Add the chicken stock and slowly bring to a boil. Add the mirin, soy sauce, garlic, and sugar. Cook for a further 1–2 minutes. Add the parsley, basil, and chives, and toss together.

Toss the angel hair with the asparagus mixture to combine. Add the truffle oil, toss together, and serve immediately.

**SERVES 4**

*Wine suggestions*
Ripe-style sauvignon blanc: 1999 Shaw & Smith Sauvignon Blanc; 1998 Preston Sauvignon Blanc; 1998 Chatelain Pouilly-Fumé

# Linguine with a Ragout of Oriental Mushrooms

*A pasta done in the Asian style, with the earthy and silky mushrooms a highlight of the dish. Use whatever mushrooms are available. I have given starter portions, so increase quantities if you're cooking as a main.*

50 g (1 1/2 oz) linguine
30 g (1 oz) shimeji mushrooms, sliced
4 shiitake mushrooms, sliced
12 oyster mushrooms, sliced
1 clove garlic, finely chopped
2 tablespoons olive oil
1 tablespoon sake
2 teaspoons mirin
1/2 tablespoon soy sauce
80 ml (2 1/2 fl oz) chicken stock
1 tablespoon julienned parsley
salt and pepper
2 tablespoons peeled and diced tomato
1 pinch chile powder
1 teaspoon black sesame seeds
chives, cut into 2 cm (3/4 in) lengths

Cook the linguine in plenty of salted boiling water until *al dente*. Drain.

Sauté the mushrooms and garlic in the olive oil. Once the mushrooms have wilted, add the sake, mirin, and soy sauce. Add the chicken stock.

When the mushrooms are cooked, add the pasta and parsley, and toss. Taste and adjust the seasoning with salt and pepper. Add the tomato, chile powder, sesame seeds, and chives. Serve immediately.

**SERVES 4**

*Wine suggestions*
Medium-bodied red: 1998 Gary Crittendon "I" Sangiovese; 1997 Dalla Valle Sangiovese Pietre Rosse; 1997 Casa Sola Chianti Classico

There is a Japanese way of thinking that looks on a piece of ceramic without food as unfinished.

But put some food on it,

and the piece has a life,

a reason to be.

## Functional, visual art

Mitsuo Shoji is one of my closest friends, and very much a part of our restaurant family. He drops by every night after work for a drink and a chat, and to check on how his other "family members" are doing.

Mitsuo's work is an important part of my work. There is a Japanese way of thinking that looks on a piece of ceramic without food as unfinished. But put some food on it, and the piece has a life, a reason to be.

The plates that Mitsuo makes for the restaurant are functional, visual art. Their texture and color are unsurpassed, and an inspiration for what I do. I try to use as much of his work as possible in the restaurant, for instance, for the oysters (see page 21), the tian of smoked ocean trout (see page 45), and the tartare of tuna and goat cheese (see page 53).

Mitsuo has lectured and demonstrated extensively throughout Europe, the US and Japan. He has had more than thirty solo exhibitions and his work is always in demand from galleries around the world. He lectures at the Sydney College of the Arts at the University of Sydney.

It's an honor for me to be able to display his work at the restaurant, and here, in the pages of this book.

"It is so exciting for me to see
Tetsuya using my ceramics in
his restaurant. I find it fascinating
to watch him create new dishes
especially for my plates."

## Testuya's 'gokiburi'

I first met Tetsuya eight years ago. I had tried for some time to book a place in his famed restaurant, so my wife and I were extremely excited when we had our first meal there. When the waitress asked me how my meal was, I commented that the sauce on the tuna was a little too sweet for me. Tetsuya came out of the kitchen to discuss this and the conversation moved from cooking techniques to ceramics. Ever since that moment we have been friends.

Fortunately for me, the Sydney College of the Arts, where I lecture, moved into the old Rozelle hospital. Now I get to drop in almost every evening to see my friend Tetsuya. As soon as I arrive, a kind waiter brings me my after-work medicine – a glass of French champagne.

It is always fascinating for me to see how Tetsuya prepares so many elegent entrée-sized courses. It's a wonderful performance to watch. So I sit and observe the construction of Tetsuya's creations and I often stay till the restaurant closes. My wife used to get cross when I wouldn't eat dinner at home afterwards, but how could I say no to a taste of this or that that Tetsuya offered me? I call myself Testuya's "gokiburi" – I'm the cockroach in his kitchen.

Testuya is a genuine artist. I admire his devotion to his cooking and his professionalism. I know he has no hesitation in scouring the country for the best produce to use in his cooking.

It is so exciting for me to see Tetsuya using my ceramics in his restaurant. I find it fascinating to watch him create new dishes especially for my plates. It is important for Japanese meals to be served with special ceramics. When I studied at Kyoto University of the Arts, we cooked all the time to examine which kind of ceramics matched particular foods.

Tetsuya and I often talk about food, plates and art at his home or mine. And yes, I have even cooked for him. I have to admit I was terrified the first time Testuya came to my house for a meal, but when he requested just a bowl of hot rice with Japanese pickles, I was relieved to say the least!

MITSUO SHOJI

# Sautéed Cuttlefish with Soba

125 g (4 oz) soba noodles
2 tablespoons grapeseed oil
2 large squid hoods, cleaned and peeled
2 tablespoons olive oil
1½ tablespoons finely chopped cilantro
1 tablespoon finely chopped green onions (scallions)
8 large snowpeas, julienned

SAUCE
125 ml (4 fl oz) chicken stock
2 tablespoons soy sauce
1 tablespoon fish sauce
1 tablespoon mirin
½ teaspoon oyster sauce
¼ clove finely chopped garlic
1 teaspoon finely chopped ginger
1 pinch superfine sugar
1 pinch white pepper

GARNISH
1 tablespoon julienned nori
1 tablespoon finely chopped parsley
baby cilantro leaves
aonori
chives, cut into 2 cm (¾ in) lengths
baby mâche or baby spinach leaves

Cook the soba noodles in boiling water. As soon as it is cooked, drain and rinse under running water to remove the starch. Toss in 1 tablespoon grapeseed oil.

To make the sauce, mix together all the ingredients.

Score the squid, then cut into strips. In a cold frying pan, add the olive oil, 1 tablespoon grapeseed oil, the sauce, squid, cilantro, and green onions. Put on the heat, and start tossing. The squid must be just cooked, but not too white, so it remains tender. Add the soba noodles and snowpeas, and toss. As soon as the soba noodles are hot, it's ready.

To serve, place the squid and soba noodles in serving bowls and ladle over the sauce. Garnish with nori, parsley, baby cilantro, aonori, chives, and mâche.

**SERVES 4**

*Wine suggestions*
Medium to full-bodied chardonnay: 1998 Château Xanadu Chardonnay;
1998 Chappellet Chardonnay; 1997 Louis Carillon Puligny-Montrachet

# Cocotte Egg with Sea Urchin and Truffle

4 quail eggs
1 heaped teaspoon finely julienned black truffle
1–2 pieces sea urchin
4 teaspoons chicken stock

GARNISH
chives, finely chopped
extra black truffle, julienned
sea salt

Break the quail eggs into small serving bowls. Mix the truffle with the sea urchin and add to the eggs. Add the stock.

Cover the bowls with plastic wrap. Set the bowls in a steamer over the lowest heat possible for a few minutes until the egg is just set. (You may need to do this in batches, depending on the size of your steamer.)

Remove the bowls from the steamer and garnish with chives, black truffle, and sea salt before serving.

**SERVES 2**

*Wine suggestions*
Aromatic dry white: 1999 Petaluma Viognier; 1998 Ojai Vineyards Viognier Roll Ranch Vineyard California; Andre Perret Condrieu "Coteaux du Chery"

# Steamed Abalone with Witlof and Peaches

*The delicate texture of abalone is a contrast to the crunch of the peaches. The truffle and black bean make an interesting combination.*

500–600 g (1 lb) abalone
1 head endive, julienned
grapeseed oil
abalone liver, thinly sliced (optional)
1 small handful arugula leaves
3–4 truffled wild peaches or green olives, thinly sliced

### SAUCE
1 tablespoon sake
2 teaspoons finely chopped salted black beans
1 pinch salt
2 tablespoons white sesame oil
150 g (5 oz) grated daikon
2 tablespoons chicken stock
½ teaspoon mirin
½ teaspoon soy sauce
zest of ¼ orange, julienned

### GARNISH
chives, cut into 2.5 cm (1 in) lengths
leek or green onions (scallions), julienned (optional)

If you are using fresh abalone, steam with some grated radish for 20 minutes over a gentle heat. Once cooked, remove from the heat, cool slightly, and slice.

If using canned abalone, you won't need to cook it at all. Slice.

To make the sauce, combine the sake, black beans, salt, sesame oil, daikon, stock, mirin, and soy sauce in a frying pan. Mix well, and adjust the seasoning to taste. Bring to a boil to get rid of the alcohol in the sake. Add the orange zest and stir through.

Sauté the endive in a little grapeseed oil until wilted. Add the abalone liver, if using.

Just before serving, wilt the arugula in the sauce.

To serve, place the endive on 4 serving plates. Fan the sliced peaches on top, then the sliced abalone. Pour over the sauce. Top with some arugula leaves, and garnish with chives and leek.

**SERVES 4**

*Wine suggestions*
Dry sauvignon blanc: 1999 Hillstowe Sauvignon Blanc; 1998 Château Souverain Sauvignon Blanc; 1998 Chatelain Sancerre

## Roasted Tasmanian Lobster with Carrot and Tarragon

4 lobsters
all-purpose flour for dusting
1 pinch white pepper
1 tablespoon olive oil
½ teaspoon finely chopped tarragon
½ tablespoon finely chopped chives
¼ clove finely chopped garlic

### CARROT PURÉE
2 medium-sized carrots, chopped
enough chicken stock to cover
salt and pepper

### GARNISH
chives, finely chopped
leek, julienned

Preheat the oven to 100°C (210°F).

Cut the lobsters in half, then along their joints. Toss in a little flour and pepper. Heat the olive oil in a frying pan, add the lobster pieces, and toss until the flesh just turns white. Place in the preheated oven for a few minutes until the shells turn red, then add the tarragon, chives, and garlic.

Cook the carrots in the stock until soft. Season with salt and pepper to taste, and purée. The mixture shouldn't be too thick – thin out with a little stock if necessary. Check the seasoning again.

Put the lobster heads in the oven to heat up until the shells turn red.

Place some lobster on each serving plate, and spoon over the carrot purée. Garnish with chives, leek, and the warmed lobster heads.

**SERVES 4**

*Wine suggestions*
Complex chardonnay: 1998 Cullens Chardonnay; 1998 Robert Mondavi Reserve Chardonnay; 1997 Lafon Meursault "Clos de la Barre"

# Steamed Snapper with Celeriac Mousse

*Serve in a bowl with a lid so that your guests can enjoy the aromas when the lid is lifted.*

4 x 30–50 g (1–1½ oz) snapper fillet, skin off
2 egg whites
100 g (3½ oz) celeriac (celery root), grated
2 tablespoons soy sauce
2 tablespoons mirin
1 tablespoon sake
200 ml (7 fl oz) chicken stock
2 teaspoons cornstarch
2 tablespoons water

GARNISH
2 okra, sliced
wakame (see page 170)
tororo konbu
aonori
chives or green onions (scallions), finely chopped
1 pinch finely julienned lemon zest or yuzu (optional)

Place the snapper in a bowl that will just fit into the steamer.

Beat the egg whites until they just turn white and start foaming. Fold with the celeriac and put on top of the fish.

Set a steamer over gently simmering water.

Cover the bowl with plastic wrap and steam the snapper over a gentle heat for 7–8 minutes or, depending on the thickness, until cooked. Insert a skewer in the center of the fish to test for doneness. Remove from the heat.

Blanch the okra and slice on an angle.

Bring the soy sauce, mirin, sake, and stock to a boil. Dissolve the cornstarch in water, and add to the mirin mixture to thicken. Stir well.

Pour the sauce on top of the fish, and garnish with the blanched okra, wakame, konbu, aonori, chives, and lemon zest, if using.

**SERVES 4**

*Wine suggestions*
Medium-bodied chardonnay: 1998 Voyager Estate Chardonnay; 1997 Matanzas Creek Chardonnay Sonoma Valley; 1997 Jean-Pierre Grossot Chablis "Vaucopan"

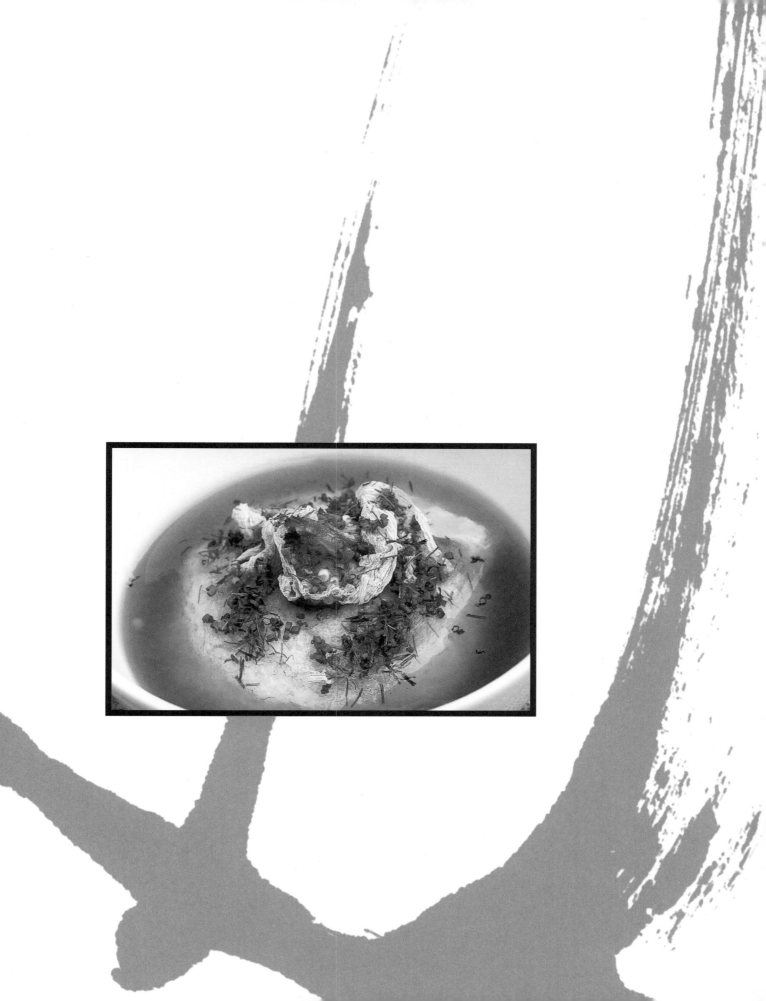

# Roasted Scampi Seasoned with Tea and Scampi Oil

*The key to this dish is to just cook the scampi – once overcooked, the flesh will turn mushy.*

10 medium-sized scampi, halved lengthwise
salt and white pepper
1 teaspoon Ceylon tea
1 tablespoon scampi oil (see pages 169–170)
½ teaspoon Banyuls vinegar or sherry vinegar
ogonori or wakame (see pages 169, 170)

GARNISH
deep-fried julienned leek
shredded nori

Preheat the oven to 260°C (500°F).

Season the scampi with salt and white pepper to taste. Grind the tea to a powder and sprinkle on top of the scampi.

Place the scampi halves on a baking tray and put in the oven for 3 minutes. As soon as the scampi feel hot to the touch, they are ready. They should be just cooked, and still look slightly translucent.

Combine the scampi oil and vinegar.

To serve, place a little ogonori on the base of the serving plates. Place the scampi halves on top, drizzle with the combined scampi oil and vinegar, and garnish with the leek and nori.

**SERVES 4**

*Wine suggestions*
Medium to full-bodied chardonnay: 1997 Marc Morey Chassagne-Montrachet "Virondot"; 1998 Stoniers Reserve Chardonnay; 1997 Château Montelena Chardonnay

# Slow-roasted Rouget with Buckwheat Vinaigrette

1 tablespoon grapeseed oil
1 tablespoon olive oil
2 teaspoons black olive paste
¼ teaspoon minced garlic
4 medium-sized snapper fillets, trimmed
1 tablespoon goat cheese
leaves from 1 bunch arugula

### BUCKWHEAT VINAIGRETTE
3 tablespoons buckwheat
1 tablespoon olive oil
1 tablespoon grapeseed oil
1 tablespoon rice wine vinegar
½ teaspoon soy sauce
½ teaspoon lemon juice
1 medium-sized tomato, peeled and finely diced

### GARNISH
12 small cape gooseberries, halved
1 tablespoon finely julienned basil
hijiki (see page 169)
1 tablespoon baby shiso or mint leaves

Preheat the oven to 160°C (325°F).

To make the vinaigrette, blanch the buckwheat in boiling water until soft. Refresh in cold water. Combine the olive and grapeseed oils, vinegar, soy sauce, and lemon juice. Add the buckwheat and tomato, and gently combine.

Combine the grapeseed and olive oils, olive paste, and garlic, and pour the mixture into a shallow baking dish. Immerse the snapper fillets in the oil and roast in the oven for 5 minutes, or until the fish is soft to the touch.

Remove the fish fillets from the oil and set aside.

To serve, place a little goat cheese in the center of serving plates. Top with 3 arugula leaves and a fish fillet. Spoon over the buckwheat vinaigrette, and garnish with cape gooseberries, basil, hijiki, and shiso leaves.

**SERVES 4**

*Wine suggestions*
Medium to full-bodied chardonnay: 1998 Plantagenet Mt Barker Chardonnay; 1998 Fisher Vineyards Chardonnay Coach Insignia; 1997 Remi Jobard Meursault "En Lurale"

# Warm Salad of Veal Sweetbreads with King Prawns

*A red wine dish, especially burgundy! The creaminess of the sweetbreads and the fabulous texture of the king prawns are a glorious combination.*

250 g (8 oz) veal sweetbreads
salt and pepper
1 tablespoon white wine vinegar
8 king prawns, peeled
all-purpose flour for dusting
1½ tablespoons grapeseed oil
4 asparagus, angle cut into 3 pieces
8 green beans, halved
2 fresh shiitake mushrooms, sliced
wakame (see page 170)
mixed mesclun leaves

### SAUCE
150 ml (5 fl oz) veal stock
1 tablespoon port
½ tablespoon Banyuls vinegar or sherry vinegar
½ teaspoon finely chopped shallots
salt and pepper
a dash of walnut oil

### GARNISH
2 tablespoons peeled, seeded and diced tomato
1 tablespoon julienned parsley
baby watercress
chives, cut into 2 cm (¾ in) lengths

Wash the sweetbreads to get rid of the blood. Place in a saucepan with cold water, a pinch of salt, and tablespoon of vinegar, and bring to a boil over medium heat. (Do not put in boiling water.) Cook 15 minutes or until cooked, then refresh under cold water. Drain and set aside.

Butterfly the prawns and remove the digestive tract. Score the prawns on a slight diagonal along the inside length.

*continued page 104*

Pat dry the sweetbreads and break up into bite-sized pieces. Dust lightly with flour and brown in ½ tablespoon of the grapeseed oil. Once cooked, set aside.

Very lightly dust the prawns with flour and cook in the same frying pan in another ½ tablespoon of the grapeseed oil. Season with a pinch each of salt and pepper.

To make the sauce, combine the veal stock, port, vinegar, and shallots. Bring to a boil, adjust the seasoning to taste, then add the walnut oil. Take off the heat.

Sauté the asparagus, beans, and mushrooms in the last of the grapeseed oil. Season with salt and pepper.

To serve, place the wakame on the base of the plate and some mesclun leaves on top. Add the prawns and sweetbreads, then the vegetables. Top with the tomato, parsley, watercress, and chives, and drizzle over a little sauce.

**SERVES 4**

*Wine suggestions*
Medium-bodied pinot noir: 1998 Spring Vale Pinot Noir; 1997 Jean-Marc Pavelot Savigny-Lès-Beaune "Narbantons"; 1998 Saintsbury Pinot Noir Carneros

# Roasted Barramundi with Bitter Greens and Truffled Peaches

*I use baby barramundi from Robarra in South Australia in this recipe.*

4 x 160 g (5½ oz) fillets sea bass, skin on and trimmed
sea salt and white pepper
4 tablespoons wakame (see page 170)
4 small truffled wild peaches or green olives, thinly sliced

SALAD
1 medium-sized endive, julienned
1 small tomato, peeled, seeded and diced
2 tablespoons julienned arugula
2 tablespoons finely chopped chives
½ teaspoon good quality sherry vinegar
½ tablespoon grapeseed oil

GARNISH
salt
cracked black pepper
4 teaspoons truffle oil

Halve each sea bass fillet and place under the broiler skin side up – not too close – so that the radiant heat cooks the fish. Season lightly with a pinch each of salt and pepper. Be careful not to overcook.

Toss together all the salad ingredients and mix well.

Place a little wakame on the base of each serving plate, put the peaches on top, and then the fish. Spoon a little salad on the side, and garnish with a little salt and cracked black pepper. Drizzle the truffle oil on top.

**SERVES 4**

*Wine suggestions*
Medium to full-bodied chardonnay: 1998 Petaluma Chardonnay; 1997 Dehlinger Chardonnay Reserve Estate Russian River ; 1997 Jean Pillot Puligny-Montrachet "Les Caillerets"

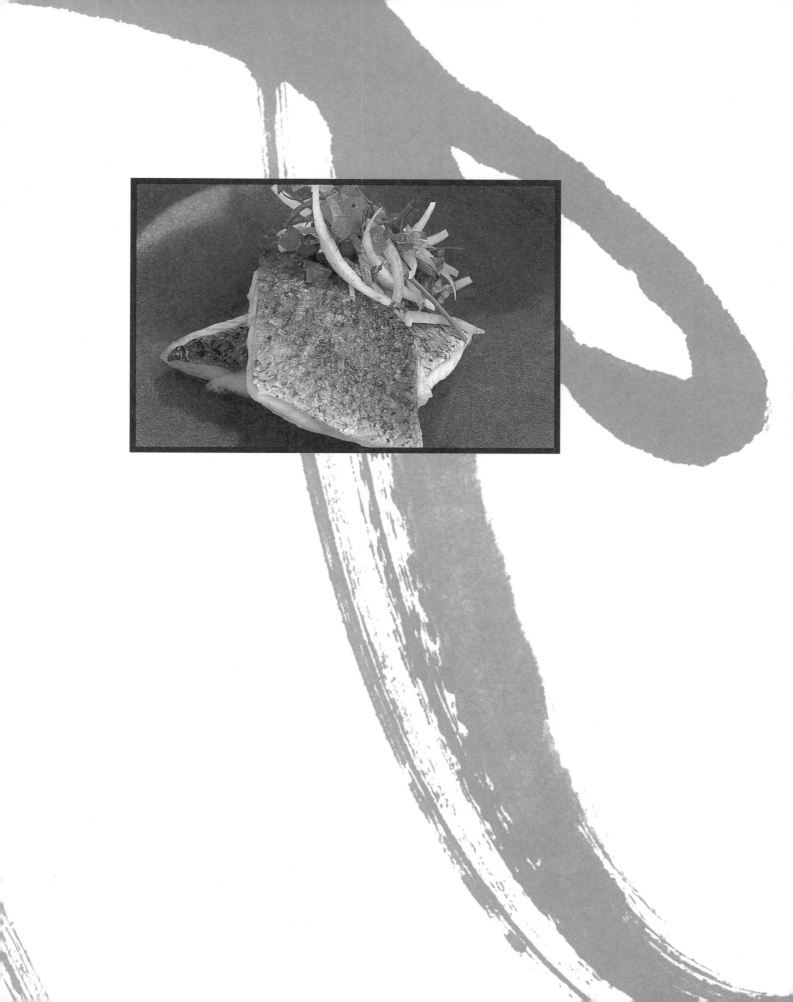

# Roasted Lobster with Braised Oxtail

1 recipe braised oxtail (see page 146)
2 heaping teaspoons sweet miso
1 shiitake mushroom, sliced
30 g (1 oz) shimeji or button mushrooms
2 tablespoons grapeseed oil
1 teaspoon mirin
2 teaspoons soy sauce
1 teaspoon sake
¼ teaspoon minced garlic
1 teaspoon finely chopped chives
lobster coral
⅓ teaspoon finely chopped tarragon
all-purpose flour
salt and white pepper to taste
1 lobster tail, halved lengthwise
1 handful spinach
wakame (see page 170)
leek, julienned

Prepare the oxtail following the instructions on page 146, omitting the sea cucumber. Debone the oxtail. Dissolve the miso in the leftover cooking liquid. Combine with the oxtail meat.

Preheat the oven to 180°C (350°F).

Sauté the mushrooms in 1 tablespoon of the grapeseed oil until wilted. Add the mirin, soy sauce, sake, garlic, and chives, then add the oxtail and miso mixture. Add the lobster coral and tarragon.

Sprinkle a little flour, salt, and pepper on the halved lobster tail and sear in a tablespoon of grapeseed oil in a frying pan, flesh side down, until it turns white. Place the tail, flesh side up, on a baking tray in the oven for 4–5 minutes to cook the center. The center should remain a little translucent, and the shells red. Remove the meat from the shells.

Blanch the spinach in boiling water.

To serve, place small mounds of wakame and spinach in a bowl. Place some oxtail, mushrooms, and juices on top. Arrange the lobster pieces on top of the oxtail, and garnish with a mound of leek.

**SERVES 4**

*Wine suggestions*
Light-bodied pinot-noir-style: 1998 Coldstream Hills Pinot Noir; 1997 Westrey Pinot Noir Willamette Valley; 1998 Domaine Robert Groffier Passetoutgrain

## The wine leads the dish

In many ways, Tetsuya's has been built by wine lovers and collectors who would bring their special bottles to enjoy with their meals. I would then design a dish or a menu to go with the wine. In this way, the wine often leads the dish. You can imagine how exciting this is for a cook, and besides, such freedom allows me the space to develop my knowledge of what to look for in a wine and in the dish that goes with it. So it's fair to say that to a large degree, my palate has been educated by these wine lovers.

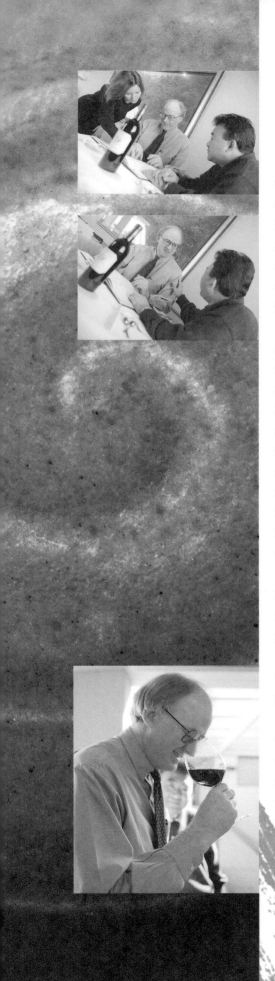

The restaurant started as a BYO – if you know how much a wine license costs in New South Wales, you know why! It was only in 1996, after Anne Willan awarded us *Gourmet Traveller* Restaurant of the Year that we obtained one. She was very wide-ranging in her praise, but one comment made me realize how we could be better. She said that a great restaurant needed a wine list of its own. And she was right. Today, more than half of the wines on our list are Australian, and the rest are French.

Over the years, I have been fortunate to encounter wine-makers and suppliers who have been very generous with their time, their knowledge and their support. My dear friend Jon Osbeiston, who has known my food since its Ultimo days, has been there along the way, pointing this or the other out to me, alerting me to something he knows I'd like. He is thoroughly familiar with my food, too, which helps! We have been through many special dinners at Tetsuya's: we both recall fondly a twelve-course dinner of Krug and caviar that started at eight in the evening and went on till the early hours of the morning. Such indulgence! Or a fourteen-course La Chapelle dinner which went on for just as long.

My approach to matching wine and food is purely instinctive. I might taste a particular wine and pick up elements that will suit a dish on the menu, or I might design a dish to go with a particular wine I have had.

I have asked Jon to choose the wines to go with the recipes in this book. There are no hard and fast rules, and the suggested matches work regardless of vintage. Jon explains his choices thus:

"I like the use of young wines with Tetsuya's food. The low tannins work well and it's a good opportunity to demonstrate each style of wine. However, with bordeaux, for example, age is necessary for them to work, to round out the tannins – they are too big when young. So they make only infrequent appearances with Tets' food. The same applies to chardonnay. I tend to stay away from the big, oaky varieties. I want the wines not to compete with but to complement the food. At the end of the day, it's balance I am looking for."

# Roasted Duck Breast with Confit Potato and Duck Jus

*Confit potatoes cooked in a bag produce a glorious, creamy result that is not too rich.*

4 x 200–250 g (7–8 oz) small duck breasts
salt and pepper
1 tablespoon grapeseed oil
50 ml (1½ fl oz) duck jus or duck stock or brown chicken stock
small handful chrysanthemum leaves
4 sprigs sansho

### GLAZE
200 ml (7 fl oz) soy sauce
4 tablespoons brown sugar
100 ml (3½ fl oz) mirin or dry sherry

### CONFIT POTATO
4 pink fir apple potatoes or any other waxy potato, peeled
½ tablespoon goose fat or a plain-flavored oil like grapeseed
1 pinch sea salt
1 pinch white pepper
1 pinch superfine sugar

To make the glaze, combine the soy sauce, brown sugar, and mirin in a saucepan and stir until the sugar dissolves. Cool.

To make the confit potato, pare the potatoes into barrel shapes. Place the potatoes in a freezer bag or heatproof bag with the goose fat, salt, pepper, and sugar. Expel all excess air and tie the top tightly. Place the bag in a pot of boiling water and cook for 30 minutes.

Preheat the oven to 150°C (300°F).

*continued page 114*

Trim the duck breasts well, season with salt and pepper to taste, and brown in batches, skin side down, in the grapeseed oil in a non-stick frying pan. When the skin is dark brown and crisp, turn to cook the flesh very briefly.

Transfer the breasts to a baking tray and place in the oven to cook for another 5–6 minutes. Remove from the oven, wrap the tray in foil and allow to rest.

Before serving, paint the breasts with the glaze and place under the broiler. Once it starts to bubble, remove, glaze, and place under the broiler again. Repeat one more time.

Reheat the duck jus and season to taste with salt and pepper.

Blanch the chrysanthemum leaves in some boiling water.

When ready to serve, place the chrysanthemum on serving plates. Remove the potato from the bags and place on top. Slice the duck breast and fan over the potato. Spoon over some duck jus and garnish with a sprig of sansho.

**SERVES 4**

### Wine suggestions
Full-bodied pinot noir: 1998 Bass Phillip Reserve Pinot Noir; 1998 J. Rochioli Pinot Noir (any vineyard); 1997 Bernard Dugat-Py Charmes-Chambertin

# Breast of Duck with Apple and Ginger Dipping Sauce

*Make the dipping sauce a few days ahead to allow the flavors to combine – it improves with keeping. I use older duck for this because it has more flavor.*

250–270 g (8–9 oz) duck breast
1 tablespoon grapeseed oil
200 ml (7 fl oz) soy sauce
100 ml (3½ fl oz) mirin
4 heaped tablespoons brown sugar

DIPPING SAUCE
3 tablespoons rice wine vinegar
200 ml (7 fl oz) soy sauce
50 ml (1½ fl oz) mirin
1 Granny Smith apple, grated
1 tablespoon grated ginger
50 ml (1½ fl oz) unsweetened apple juice
½ white onion, grated
1 clove garlic, grated
1 pinch white pepper

GARNISH
baby leeks, julienned
grapeseed oil
black sesame seeds

Pan-fry the duck, skin side down, in ½ tablespoon grapeseed oil, until the skin is crispy and brown. Depending on the size of the duck, you might have to finish the cooking in the oven. The duck should be just cooked.

Combine the soy sauce, mirin, and brown sugar. Paint this glaze on the duck once it has come out of the oven, and slide under the broiler, skin side up, to brown lightly. Take the duck out from under the broiler, glaze, and broil again. Repeat one more time, taking care to remove the duck before burning. Rest for 7–8 minutes, covered with foil.

To make the dipping sauce, combine all the ingredients and mix well.

Pan-fry the leeks in another ½ tablespoon grapeseed oil.

To serve, slice the duck breast and place on a plate with the leeks. Place the dipping sauce in a bowl. Sprinkle some black sesame seeds on the surface of the sauce.

**SERVES 4**

*Wine suggestions*
Medium to full-bodied pinot noir: 1998 Barrat Pinot Noir; 1997 Sanford Pinot Noir; 1997 Michel Gros Vosne-Romanée "Clos des Reas"

## Duck Terrine

*Taste the mixture before you cook it, to make sure that it's adequately seasoned. The terrine can keep for a week to ten days, and the taste actually improves with keeping.*

200 g (7 oz) chicken, minced
200 g (7 oz) pork, minced
400 g (14 oz) duck leg, minced
zest of ½ orange
1 tablespoon goose fat
1 teaspoon mirin
1 teaspoon soy sauce
salt and pepper to taste
1 teaspoon finely chopped thyme
2 teaspoons finely chopped sage
1 teaspoon finely chopped rosemary
1 teaspoon ground ginger

Combine all the ingredients in a bowl and, using your hands (wear gloves), squeeze the mixture very well, until the ingredients are well mixed and the paste is sticky.

Place a sheet of plastic wrap on a chopping board. Spoon some of the paste in the bottom third, and roll up, using the plastic wrap to move the paste, like you roll sushi. Squeeze the roll so it forms a sausage shape and twist both ends of the film to seal tightly.

Place the roll on some foil, roll up and twist to seal the ends. Repeat with the remaining mixture.

Set a steamer over medium heat and gently steam the rolls for 30 minutes. If the steamer gets too hot, open the lid to release the excess steam.

Test for doneness – the surface of the roll should be just firm when cooked.

Remove the rolls from the steamer, allow to cool, and set aside at least overnight in the refrigerator. Slice before serving.

**MAKES TWO TO THREE 5 CM (2 IN) DIAMETER ROLLS**

*Wine suggestions*
Cabernet sauvignon: 1997 Moss Wood Cabernet Sauvignon; 1996 Silver Oak Alexander Valley Cabernet Sauvignon; 1995 Château Lagrange (St-Julien)

## Roasted Squab with Buckwheat, Shimeji and Shiitake

4 tablespoons buckwheat
4 x 450–500 g (13–16 oz) squab
salt and white pepper
grapeseed oil
1 teaspoon finely chopped shallots
¼ teaspoon finely minced garlic
40 g (1½ oz) shimeji or button mushrooms
2 medium-sized shiitake mushrooms, sliced
30 g (1 oz) chestnut mushrooms
1 tablespoon sake
50 ml (1½ fl oz) chicken stock
50 ml (1½ fl oz) veal stock
1 teaspoon soy sauce
1 teaspoon mirin
1 handful spinach

GARNISH
deep-fried julienned leek
chives, cut into 2 cm (¾ in) lengths

Blanch the buckwheat in some salted boiling water for about 5 minutes, or until soft but not completely cooked. Drain and refresh under cool running water. Set aside until ready to use.

Preheat the oven to 250°C (475°F).

Cut off the squab wing tips and legs, and stuff in the cavity. Stuff in a paper towel to absorb any excess moisture. Pat the squab dry and season with salt and pepper to taste.

*continued page 122*

Pour some grapeseed oil into a frying pan so that it is 1–2 cm (¼–½ in) deep. Brown the skin of the squab in the oil. Once the skin is brown but not crisp, transfer the squab to a baking tray and place in the oven for 5 minutes to finish cooking. Remove from the oven, wrap in foil and rest for at least 15 minutes.

Heat ½ tablespoon grapeseed oil in a frying pan and add the shallots and garlic. Add the mushrooms. Sauté until the mushrooms soften, then add the sake, both stocks, soy sauce, mirin, and salt and pepper to taste. Add the buckwheat and toss. Lower the heat.

Blanch the spinach in boiling water.

To serve, take the breasts off the squab and slice into 3–4 pieces. Place a mound of spinach on the base of each serving plate. Put the squab legs on top, then spoon on some of the mushroom and buckwheat mixture. Fan the squab breast over the top. Garnish with leek and chives.

**SERVES 4**

*Wine suggestions*
A rich pinot noir: 1997 Tarrawarra Pinot Noir; 1998 Andersons Conn Valley Vineyard Pinot Noir "Valhalla Vineyard"; 1997 Domaine Robert Groffier Chambolle-Musigny "Les Sentiers"

# Seared Swordfish with Artichoke and Olive

*Tuna or marlin can be used in place of the swordfish. If you can find sundried tomato paste, add 1 teaspoon of it onto the finished dish.*

4 x 50–70 g (1½–2½ oz) swordfish fillets
½ teaspoon grapeseed oil
2 large artichokes
lemon juice
salt
wakame (see page 170)

### SAUCE
1 teaspoon soy sauce
1 teaspoon mirin
80 ml (2½ fl oz) olive oil
1½ teaspoons black olive paste
¼ teaspoon finely chopped garlic
2 tablespoons chicken stock

### GARNISH
arugula leaves
parsley, finely chopped
green onions (scallions), julienned
2 tablespoons peeled and diced tomato

Preheat the oven to 130°–140°C (275°F).

Sear the swordfish on both sides in the oil in a non-stick frying pan over high heat. Transfer to the oven for a few minutes to help cook through. I prefer to serve the fish medium-rare.

Trim the artichokes and cut in half. Remove the hairy choke, cut into quarters, and cook in some water with lemon juice and salt until tender.

To make the sauce, combine all the ingredients in a saucepan and gently heat.

Just before serving, wilt the arugula in the sauce.

To serve, place the wakame on warm serving plates, followed by the swordfish. Place a quarter of artichoke on the side, and garnish with parsley, green onions, arugula, and tomato.

**SERVES 4**

*Wine suggestions*
A full-bodied rosé or light red: 2000 Charles Melton Rosé of Virginia; 1998 Berringer Nouveau California; 1999 Domaine Tempier Bandol Rosé

# Roasted Quail Breast with Gobo and Black Truffle

*Gobo is the Japanese name for burdock. It is a root much used in Japanese cooking. If gobo is not available you can use salsify as a substitute. The earthiness of the gobo enhances the taste of the black truffle.*

1 small daikon
500 ml (16 fl oz) water
1 x 5 cm (2 in) piece konbu
1 tablespoon soy sauce
½ tablespoon mirin
4 quail breasts, the largest you can get
1 tablespoon grapeseed oil
2 heaped tablespoons fresh soy beans
1 handful spinach

SAUCE
200 ml (7 fl oz) chicken stock
½ teaspoon port
1 tablespoon finely chopped gobo
salt and black pepper
1 teaspoon finely chopped black truffle, or as much as you like

GARNISH
black truffle, thinly sliced
chives, cut into 2 cm (¾ in) lengths
parsley, julienned

Cut the daikon into 4 rounds of about 2 cm (¾ in) thickness. Pare the edges so that they do not break during cooking. In a saucepan, combine the daikon with the water, konbu, soy sauce, and mirin and cook until the daikon is tender.

Preheat the oven to 80–90°C (200°F).

Sear the quail breasts, skin side down, in the grapeseed oil in a frying pan, and place in the oven for 5 minutes.

To make the sauce, reduce the chicken stock and port with the gobo to 80 ml (2½ fl oz). Add salt and black pepper to taste. Add the truffle.

Blanch the soy beans and spinach separately in plenty of salted boiling water until tender.

To serve, place a small mound of spinach on the plate. Put a round of daikon on top, and the quail breast on top of the daikon. Spoon over the sauce and place a few soy beans on the side. Garnish with truffle, chives, and parsley.

**SERVES 4**
*Wine suggestions*

Grenache-based red: 1998 Clarendon Hills "Clarendon Hills" Grenache; 1997 Bonny Doon "Le Cigar Volant"; 1998 Clos du Caillou Châteauneuf-du-Pape

## Quail Legs with Ginger and Five-spice Powder

200 ml (7 fl oz) grapeseed oil
12 quail legs
$\frac{1}{2}$ clove garlic, thinly sliced
salt and pepper
1 pinch superfine sugar
$\frac{1}{3}$ teaspoon five-spice powder
1 drop sesame oil
1 drop soy sauce
$\frac{1}{2}$ teaspoon mirin

GARNISH
green onions (scallions), julienned
ginger, julienned

Heat the grapeseed oil in a wok or frying pan and toss the quail legs with the garlic for 5–6 minutes or until tender and lightly browned, Drain on paper towels. Discard the oil.

Return the quail to the wok or pan and dry toss with salt and pepper to taste, sugar, five-spice powder, sesame oil, soy sauce, and mirin. When all the flavors are well combined, transfer to a serving plate.

Serve garnished with green onions and ginger.

**SERVES 4**

*Wine suggestions*
Medium-bodied shiraz or zinfandel: 1998 Chapoutier Crozes-Hermitage "Les Meysonniers"; 1998 Chapoutier Australia Shiraz; 1997 Ravenswood Napa Zinfandel

# Slow-roasted Rack of Lamb with Miso and Blue Cheese

2 medium-sized endive, cut into quarters lengthwise
500 ml (16 fl oz) chicken stock
5 tablespoons grapeseed oil
1 pinch superfine sugar
sea salt and white pepper
4 small racks of lamb with 6 cutlets per rack, trimmed of all fat
1 large bunch thyme
1 large bunch snowpea leaves

### SAUCE
100 g (3½ oz) Japanese white miso paste
15 g (½ oz) blue cheese
1 teaspoon soy sauce
1 teaspoon mirin
1 teaspoon grated ginger

### GARNISH
1 tablespoon finely chopped green onions (scallions)
1 tablespoon finely chopped chives
1 teaspoon black sesame seeds
1 teaspoon roasted white sesame seeds

Preheat the oven to 220°C (425°F).

Place the endive in a small baking dish and cover two-thirds of the way with chicken stock. Add 2 tablespoons of the grapeseed oil and season with a pinch of sugar, sea salt, and white pepper to taste. Cover with foil and cook for 1 hour in the oven. Remove from the oven when the endive is tender and set aside, covered.

Reduce the oven temperature to 130°C (175°F) to cook the lamb.

Season the outside of each lamb rack with salt and pepper to taste.

Heat the remaining 3 tablespoons of the grapeseed oil in a frying pan until it gives off a haze, and sear the lamb quickly over high heat until golden.

Remove the lamb from the frying pan and place in a roasting pan with thyme sprigs under each lamb rack. Place in the oven and roast for 30–40 minutes, or until cooked to your preference.

*continued page 132*

Meanwhile, bring the remaining chicken stock to a boil, reduce to a simmer and add the miso paste. Stir until completely dissolved. Add the blue cheese and continue to stir until dissolved and sauce thickens. Add the soy sauce, mirin, and ginger, stirring constantly. Remove from the heat and strain the sauce through a fine-meshed sieve. Taste and adjust the seasoning.

Once the lamb is cooked, remove from the oven. Remove the meat from each rack in one piece by slicing lengthwise along the bone. Discard the bones and cut the lamb into thick medallions.

Blanch the snowpea leaves in boiling water.

To serve, arrange the snowpea leaves in the center of serving plates. Top with the endive and lamb medallions. Spoon over the miso sauce. Garnish with green onions and chives, and sprinkle with the sesame seeds.

**SERVES 4–6**

*Wine suggestions*
Medium to full-bodied spicy red: 1998 Mount Langi Ghiran Shiraz; 1997 Ridge "Geyserville"; 1997 Thierry Allemand Cornas "Reynaud"

# Snapper with Clams and Saffron

*A hearty dish that is delicious served with rice or bread. The tomato sauce recipe makes more than enough for this dish. The leftover sauce can be used for pasta.*

TOMATO SAUCE
60 ml (2 fl oz) olive oil
¼ medium-sized onion, chopped
¼ stalk celery, finely chopped
1 clove garlic, chopped
7 small ripe tomatoes, chopped
½ tablespoon tomato paste
60 ml (2 fl oz) dry white wine
salt and pepper

2 medium-sized snapper
1 tablespoon olive oil
400 g (14 oz) clams, purged
3 cloves garlic, chopped
2 small red chiles, seeded and finely chopped
1 teaspoon finely chopped anchovy fillets
60 ml (2 fl oz) tomato sauce (this page)
1 pinch saffron threads, or to taste
200 ml (7 fl oz) water
3 tablespoons finely chopped parsley
salt and pepper

To make the tomato sauce, heat the olive oil in a frying pan and sauté the onion, celery, and garlic over low heat, stirring occasionally, until soft. Add the tomatoes, tomato paste, and white wine, and simmer over medium heat for 10–15 minutes until thick and pulpy. Season to taste with salt and pepper.

Chop the tails and fins off the fish and cut a deep cross through the thickest part on each side, down to the bone. (This prevents the skin from bursting during cooking.)

Heat 1 tablespoon olive oil in a frying pan and cook the fish over medium heat for 2 minutes, turning once. Add the clams, garlic, chile, anchovies, tomato sauce, saffron, and water to the pan, and cook over medium heat for 10 minutes until the clams open and the fish is tender. To test, push the tongs into the cross on the fish. If the flesh comes away from the bone, it is cooked.

Remove the fish and clams with a slotted spoon and place in 2 warm, deep bowls. Add the sauce and garnish with parsley.

**SERVES 2 AS A MAIN COURSE**

*Wine suggestions*
Sauvignon blanc with good ripeness: 1999 Lenswood Sauvignon Blanc; 1998 Flora Springs Wine Co. Sauvignon Blanc Soliloquy; 1998 Jean-Max Roger Sancerre "Cuvée CC"

# Grilled Fillet of Veal with Wasabi and Sea Urchin Butter

*I prefer using slightly darker veal for this dish, one that has been on grass for 4–6 weeks.*
*To me it is tender and tastes better.*

WASABI AND SEA URCHIN BUTTER
5 tablespoons wasabi powder
250 g (8 oz) unsalted butter
60 g (2 oz) sea urchin roe
2 tablespoons finely chopped chives
2 teaspoons finely chopped tarragon
1/2 teaspoon finely chopped thyme
2 tablespoons light soy sauce
2 teaspoons lemon juice
1 pinch cayenne pepper

4 x 80–100 g (3–3 1/2 oz) veal medallions
2 teaspoons olive oil

GARNISH
4–5 tablespoons wakame (see page 170)
4–5 tablespoons hijiki (see page 169)
4–5 tablespoons finely shaved cucumber
2 tablespoons pickled ginger

To make the wasabi and sea urchin butter, in a food processor fitted with a paddle, combine all the ingredients and beat. Be careful not to over-beat. Keep as white as possible. Spread the mixture on the bottom third of a piece of wax paper or foil and roll up. Freeze until required.

Pan-fry the veal in the olive oil until lightly brown (medium-rare).

Remove the butter from the freezer and cut into 8 x 5 mm (1/4 in) slices. Place the butter on the veal medallions and cook under a very hot broiler until the top is golden brown.

To serve, place the veal on serving plates and garnish with the wakame and hijiki. Place a mound of cucumber and ginger on the side.

**SERVES 4**

*Wine suggestions*
Medium to full-bodied shiraz: 1998 Cape Jaffa Shiraz; 1997 Joseph Phelps Vin de Mistral Syrah; 1998 Domaine Combier Crozes-Hermitage

To Tetsuya
In Admiration of Your Talent
Your Friend—Ottmar

## My life is the restaurant

The restaurant is my life and my home. Or, to put it another way, my life is the restaurant.

Not surprisingly, because of the hours I spend there and because I live much of my life through the restaurant, I consider the people who work, eat, and play there my family. Many of the regular patrons are now my personal friends, and their loyalty and support mean a lot to me. I hope they have found their dining experience special, and see the food as an extension of my personal esteem of their friendship.

Many of my staff have been with me a long while. It takes those who work with me in the kitchen a long time to get what I do, and it is my hope that I provide them with the guidance and teaching they look for. It gives me joy to see them grow and develop as accomplished cooks.

The restaurant's suppliers are a long-suffering bunch who know what happens when I don't get exactly what I want. Through the years we have argued and fought when things were not quite right. But that's what family members do, isn't it?

I am but a humble cook. My pleasure comes from their pleasure; my happiness from theirs.

# Venison with Roasted Shallots and Morels

*We make this dish in small portions in the restaurant, but you can increase the quantities and serve it as a main.*

16 dried morels
4 shallots
3 tablespoons grapeseed oil
salt and pepper
1 potato, quartered
250 ml (8 fl oz) chicken stock
½ tablespoon soy sauce
½ tablespoon mirin
1 x 10 cm (4 in) piece konbu
4 x 40–50 g (1½ oz) venison
1 pinch ground sansho or szechuan pepper
1 handful spinach

SAUCE
200 ml (7 fl oz) veal stock
200 ml (7 fl oz) port
½ teaspoon soy sauce
3 tablespoons morel soaking liquid

Soak the morels in water at least 3–4 hours before cooking. In your initial rinse, wash well to remove all the grit and dirt. Keep the soaking liquid for the sauce.

Roast the shallots in 2 tablespoons of the grapeseed oil, in an oven preheated to 120°C (250°F), for 20–30 minutes or until tender. Add salt and pepper to taste.

Pare the potatoes into batons about the size of your thumb. Cook in the stock with the soy sauce, mirin, some salt, and konbu until soft.

*continued page 142*

To make the sauce, reduce the veal stock to 80 ml (2½ fl oz). In a separate pan, reduce the port to 50 ml (1½ fl oz) – it should be syrup-like. Combine the stock, port, soy sauce, and morel soaking liquid and bring to a boil. Set aside until ready to use.

Season the venison with salt, pepper, and ground sansho. In a hot frying pan (but not smoking) add 1 tablespoon grapeseed oil and sear on both sides. (I serve venison rare, but cook it more if you like.) Rest and slice in half.

Blanch the spinach in some boiling water.

Squeeze excess liquid from the morels and heat in the sauce.

To serve, place a mound of spinach in the middle of each serving plate. Put a piece of potato and shallot on top, followed by the venison and morels. Spoon over the sauce.

**SERVES 4**

*Wine suggestions*
Cabernet sauvignon: 1998 Ralph Fowler Cabernet Sauvignon; 1996 Spottswoode Cabernet Sauvignon; 1996 Château Legrange

# Pan-fried Duck Foie Gras with Rice, Honey and Soy

*A very satisfying and rich dish.*

AVOCADO PURÉE
½ avocado, peeled and sectioned
100 ml (3½ fl oz) milk
salt and cracked black pepper
1 teaspoon finely chopped chives

SAUCE
½ tablespoon honey
50 ml (1½ fl oz) soy sauce
1 teaspoon lemonade fruit juice or lemon juice

4 x 30 g (1 oz) duck foie gras
1 tablespoon grapeseed oil
8 tablespoons steamed short-grain rice
¼ avocado, finely diced

GARNISH
crushed sesame seeds
chives, cut into 2 cm (¾ in) lengths

To make the avocado purée, blend together the avocado and milk. Add salt and black pepper to taste, and then the chives.

To make the sauce, bring all the ingredients to a boil.

Slice the foie gras in half and seal on both sides in a hot pan in the grapeseed oil.

Mix the rice with the diced avocado.

To serve, place 2 tablespoons of the rice and avocado mixture in the base of each serving bowl. Spoon on a little avocado purée and add the foie gras. Spoon on some sauce and garnish with the sesame seeds and chives.

**SERVES 4**

*Wine suggestions*
Sweet but not heavy white: 1998 Yalumba Botrytis Viognier Noble Pick; 1997 Kunde Estate Winery Muscat Canelli Late Harvest; 1997 Yves Cuilleron Condrieu "Ayguets"

# Braised Oxtail with Sea Cucumber and Vegetables

1 piece sea cucumber
4 joints oxtail
1.5–2 L (4 pints) chicken stock
1 x 15 cm (6 in) piece konbu
100 ml (3½ fl oz) soy sauce
salt and pepper
8 whole baby carrots
8 whole baby turnips
1 handful chrysanthemum leaves

GARNISH
chives, cut into 2 cm (¾ in) lengths
green onions (scallions), julienned
parsley, julienned
ginger, julienned
yuzu kosho (Japanese chile and citrus paste)

You will need to soak the sea cucumber for 2–3 days, changing the water every day. The sea cucumber has to be very soft to the touch. Slice.

Bring lightly salted water to a boil and blanch the oxtail pieces to remove the excess fat. Wash under cold running water.

Combine the oxtail, sea cucumber, chicken stock, konbu, and soy sauce in a pot and cook over low heat for 1 hour or until the oxtail and sea cucumber are tender. If possible, cool overnight in the stock.

The next day, skim off the fat and debone the oxtail. Gently reheat in the stock, and season to taste with salt and pepper.

Blanch the carrots, turnips, and chrysanthemum leaves separately in boiling water.

To serve, place some chrysanthemum in the base of 4 serving bowls. Spoon on the oxtail and sea cucumber, and some stock. Divide the vegetables between the serving bowls, and garnish with the chives, green onions, parsley, and ginger. If you like, you can serve some yuzu kosho on the side.

**SERVES 4**

*Wine suggestions*
Rich, full-flavored red: 1998 Charles Melton "Nine Popes"; 1997 Joseph Phelps "Le Mistral"; 1997 Andre Brunel Châteauneuf-du-Pape "Les Cailloux"

# Braised Ox Cheek with Carrot Purée and Spring Vegetables

2 ox cheeks, approximately 400 g (14 oz) each
all-purpose flour for dusting
1 tablespoon grapeseed oil
approximately 1 L (2 pints) chicken stock
100 ml (3½ fl oz) soy sauce
1 leek, halved
2 stalks celery, left whole
200 ml (7 fl oz) sake
2 medium-sized carrots, whole
sea salt and white pepper
4–6 asparagus, halved
6 snowpeas
12 butter beans, halved
3–4 baby carrots
1 large handful spinach

Clean the ox cheeks and cut into 4 pieces. Lightly dust with some flour and brown in the grapeseed oil in a frying pan. Transfer the browned pieces to a stockpot and cover with the chicken stock, soy sauce, leek, celery, and sake. Add the medium-sized carrots.

Once the carrots are soft, remove from the pot and purée in a food processor. Adjust the purée to your desired consistency with more stock. Add salt and pepper to taste.

Keep cooking the ox cheeks over a low flame until tender, taking care not to overcook.

Remove the cheeks from the pot and place on a plate. Cover with another plate and weigh down the ox cheeks.

Blanch the asparagus, snowpeas, beans, baby carrots, and spinach separately.

To serve, place a little spinach at the base of each plate. Top with the ox cheek and spoon over some carrot purée. Place the asparagus, snowpeas, beans, and baby carrots on top, and spoon over some sauce.

**SERVES 4**

*Wine suggestions*
Medium to full-bodied shiraz: 1998 Bannockburn Shiraz; 1997 Edward St John "Durell Vineyard" Shiraz; 1997 René Rostaing Côte Rôtie

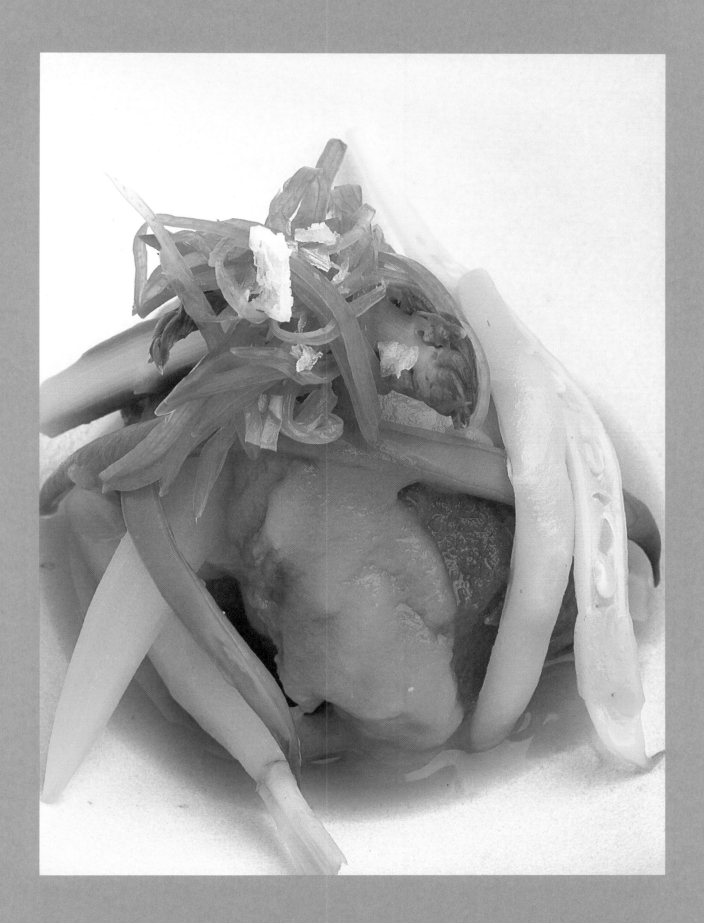

## Braised Pig's Cheek with Gobo

*Gobo (burdock) is a root much used in Japanese cooking. You can substitute salsify if gobo is not available. This is an earthy dish.*

8 pig's cheeks, skinned, cleaned and quartered
½ tablespoon grapeseed oil
600 ml (1 pint) veal stock
600 ml (1 pint) chicken stock
50 ml (1½ fl oz) port
200 ml (7 fl oz) sake
4 tablespoons soy sauce
2 tablespoons mirin
150 g (5 oz) gobo, sliced on the diagonal

GARNISH
1 small handful mizuna
green onions (scallions), sliced

Place all the ingredients in a pot and bring to a boil. Place a piece of wax paper on the surface, weigh down with a lid that is slightly smaller than the pot, and gently cook over a low heat for 45 minutes to 1 hour, or until the cheeks are tender.

Blanch the mizuna in boiling water.

To serve, place the pig's cheek and gobo in serving dishes and spoon over some of the juices. Top with mizuna and some green onions.

**SERVES 4**

*Wine suggestions*
Medium to full-bodied grenache-based: 1998 Torbreck "Steading"; 1997 Zaca Mesa Cuvée Z Santa Barara County; 1998 Domaine de la Janasse Châteauneuf-du-Pape

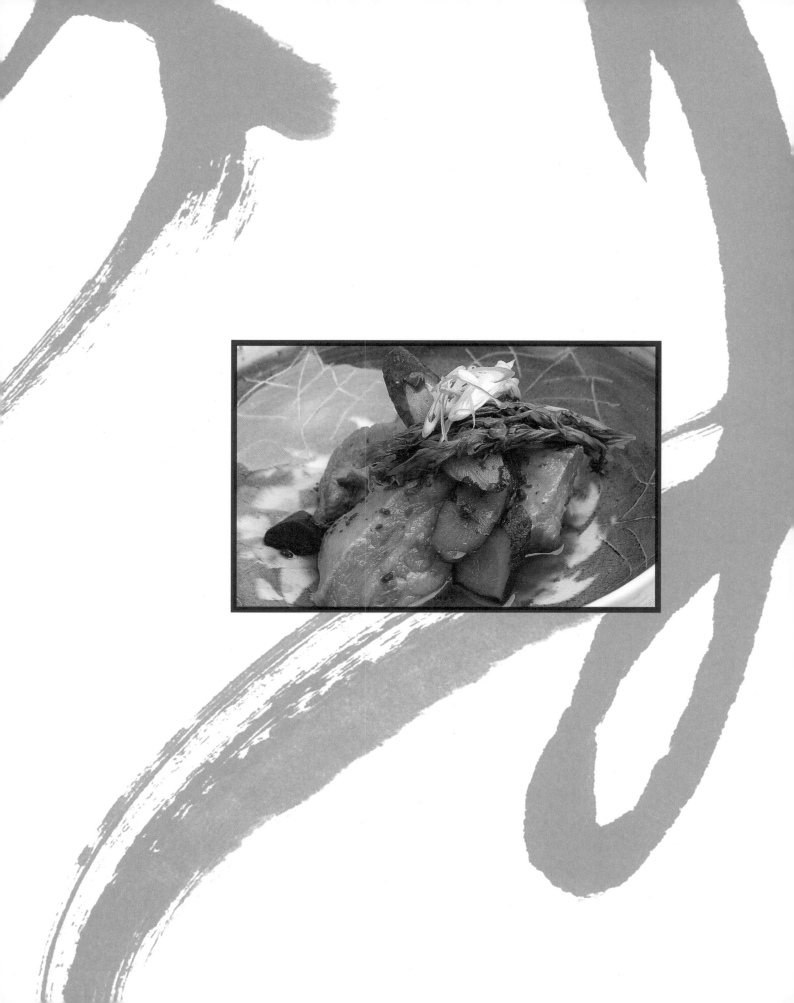

# Double-cooked Deboned Spatchcock with Bread Sauce

*Guinea fowl and bacon fat are terrific in place of the poussin and goose fat.*

4 x 125 g (4 oz) poussin breast and thigh, deboned
120 ml (4 fl oz) goose fat
½ teaspoon salt
½ teaspoon white pepper
1 pinch superfine sugar
1 pinch sea salt
500 ml (16 fl oz) chicken stock
2 leeks, cut into 15 cm (6 in) lengths
100 g (3½ oz) spinach leaves
100 g (3½ oz) fresh soy beans or broad beans
4 small pink fir apple potatoes or other waxy potatoes, peeled and boiled

### CHICKEN JUS
500 ml (16 fl oz) chicken stock
150 ml (5 fl oz) port
1 pinch salt
2 teaspoons soy sauce
½ teaspoon walnut oil

### BREAD SAUCE
6 slices white bread, crusts removed
1 clove garlic
pinch of salt
pinch of white pepper
pinch of sugar
250 ml (8 fl oz) grapeseed oil

### PARSLEY OIL
30 g (1 oz) parsley leaves
2½ tablespoons grapeseed oil

### DAIKON
1 medium-sized daikon, peeled and left whole
500 ml (16 fl oz) chicken stock
1 pinch salt
1 x 4 cm (1½ in) piece konbu

*continued page 154*

Wrap the skin of the poussin around the base of the bone to form a plump leg. Place a poussin in the corner of a freezer bag and spoon over a quarter of the goose fat. Season with salt, pepper, and sugar. Expel all air from the freezer bag and secure tightly. Repeat with the rest of the birds.

Bring a saucepan of water to 70°C (140°F) – test with a thermometer – and lower the bags with the poussin into the water. Put a lid on – this makes sure they don't float to the top. Cook for 35 minutes. Test by pushing your finger into the poussin – it should just go into the flesh. Once cooked, open the bag and allow to rest. Remove the poussin, season this time with sea salt and place under a hot broiler until golden brown.

To make the chicken jus, reduce the chicken stock by one-third over high heat, add the port, and reduce to a syrup. Stir in the salt, soy sauce, and walnut oil. Set aside.

To make the bread sauce, place all the ingredients except the oil in a food processor and process until crumbed. Slowly drizzle in the oil and process until a thick paste forms. Set aside.

To make the parsley oil, place the parsley leaves into a blender and slowly add the oil. Blend until a smooth liquid forms. Set aside.

To prepare the daikon, place all ingredients in a saucepan, cover with a sheet of wax paper under the lid (this minimizes any vibration) and bring to a boil, then lower the heat and cook until tender. Remove the daikon and slice into 1 cm (½ in) thick discs.

Heat the chicken stock and add the leek. Poach until tender, remove and slice thinly.

Blanch the spinach and soy beans in boiling water.

Divide the spinach between the serving plates. Place some daikon on top, then the poussin, leek, and chicken jus. Drizzle with parsley oil and sprinkle with soy beans. Place the potato and two teaspoons of the bread sauce to the side.

**SERVES 4**

*Wine suggestions*
Full-bodied pinot noir: 1997 Domaine A Pinot Noir; 1997 Domaine Carneros Pinot Noir Carneros; 1997 Jean Grivot Vosne-Romanée "Beaux Monts"

## Sushi of Seared Veal with Soy and Mirin Glaze

200 g (7 oz) veal fillets
½ tablespoon grapeseed oil
salt and white pepper
4 heaped tablespoons steamed sushi rice
½ teaspoon grated horseradish

SAUCE
50 ml (1½ fl oz) soy sauce
50 ml (1½ fl oz) mirin
1 teaspoon grapeseed oil
1 drop white sesame oil

GARNISH
4 sprigs chervil
½ teaspoon black olive paste

Sear the veal in the grapeseed oil until the flesh turns white, but without the top developing a crust. Rest until it comes to room temperature. Season to taste with salt and pepper.

To make the sauce, combine all the ingredients in a mixing bowl.

Take a heaping tablespoon of rice and form a ball. Put the veal on the rice and paint on some sauce. Top with some grated horseradish and garnish with a chervil sprig and a little black olive paste. Repeat with the rest of the ingredients.

**SERVES 4**

*Wine suggestions*
Light-bodied pinot noir or gamay: 1998 Diamond Valley Pinot Noir; 1998 Cartlidge and Brown Pinot Noir; 1998 Duboeuf Fleurie "Domaine des Quatre Vents"

## Granny Smith Apple Sorbet with Sauternes Jelly

### SORBET
8 large Granny Smith apples, quartered and cored (skins on)
150 ml (5 fl oz) sugar syrup (see page 170)
1 tablespoon lemon juice

### SAUTERNES JELLY
3½ envelopes gelatin
750 ml (25 fl oz) Sauternes

To make the sorbet, place the apple quarters in a food processor and blend until smooth. Strain the apple juice through a fine-meshed sieve. Measure – you should have 600 ml (1 pint).

Mix together the strained apple juice, sugar syrup, and lemon juice. Taste and adjust the sweetness to your palate by adding a little extra syrup if necessary. Pour the liquid into an ice cream machine and churn according to the manufacturer's instructions.

To make the Sauternes jelly, soak the gelatin in some cold water to soften.

Slowly bring the Sauternes to a boil in a large saucepan to burn off the alcohol. Set aside to cool a little.

Squeeze out the excess water from the gelatin and stir into the Sauternes until dissolved.

Pour the mixture through a fine-meshed sieve. Cover and refrigerate 3–4 hours or until set.

To serve, break up the jelly and place in the base of a small shot glass. Top with the sorbet and serve immediately.

**SERVES 8–10**

*There are no wine suggestions for this dish as it is a palate cleanser.*

## Lime and Ginger Crème Brûlée

600 ml (20 fl oz) heavy cream
1 vanilla bean
7 egg yolks
3 tablespoons superfine sugar
1½ tablespoons lime juice
zest of 1 lime
2 tablespoons finely grated ginger
3 tablespoons brown sugar

Combine the cream and vanilla bean in a saucepan and slowly bring to a boil.

In a stainless steel mixing bowl, whisk the egg yolks and sugar until light and fluffy. Add the lime juice, zest, and ginger, and continue to whisk together thoroughly.

Gradually pour the cream into the egg mixture, whisking continually.

Place the mixing bowl over a saucepan of boiling water and stir until the mixture thickens and coats the back of a spoon.

Remove from the heat and strain the mixture through a fine-meshed sieve. Ladle the mixture into individual ramekins and refrigerate until completely set.

To serve, sieve brown sugar on top of the crème brûlée and place under a hot broiler until the sugar caramelizes.

**SERVES 4**

*Wine suggestions*
1996 McWilliams Riverina Botrytis Semillon; 1996 Château Lafaurie Peyraguey, Sauternes; 1997 Berringer Nightingale

# Flourless Chocolate Cake

*We serve the flourless chocolate cake with bitter chocolate sorbet and orange ice cream at the restaurant. The recipes for these are included in the following pages.*

50 g (¼ cup) dark chocolate chips
20 g (2 tablespoons) cocoa powder
20 g (2 tablespoons) cornstarch
50 g (¼ cup) unsalted butter
40 g (2½ tablespoons) superfine sugar
4 medium-sized eggs, separated
a pinch of salt
¼ teaspoon cream of tartar
extra cocoa powder for dusting
whipped cream
8 mint leaves

Preheat the oven to 200°C (375°F). Grease and flour a 24 cm x 9 cm (9½ in x 3½ in) loaf pan.

Melt the chocolate in the top of a double boiler or over a pan of gently simmering water. Set aside to cool.

Combine the cocoa powder and cornstarch and sift through a fine-meshed sieve three times to make sure it is well mixed.

In a bowl fitted with an electric mixer, whisk the butter until light and creamy. Add half the sugar and continue to whisk for 3–4 minutes. Add the egg yolks to the mixture, combine well, then whisk on high for a further 3 minutes.

In another bowl, mix the melted chocolate gently to make sure it is smooth.

Whisk the egg whites with the remaining sugar, a pinch of salt, and cream of tartar until soft peaks form. Fold in one-third of the cocoa mixture, then gently fold in the remainder.

Fold the egg whites into the melted chocolate, then the butter and egg yolks mixture. Do not over-mix. Gently spoon into the prepared pan. Place the pan in a baking dish half-filled with water and bake for 30 minutes or until a skewer inserted into the middle comes out clean. Cool the cake in the pan.

To serve, slice the cake thinly and dust with cocoa powder.

Serve with a small scoop of chocolate sorbet (see page 164), orange ice cream (see page 165) and whipped cream. Decorate with fresh mint leaves.

**SERVES 6–8**

*Wine suggestions*
NV Chambers "Rosewood" Old Vines Muscadelle; 1998 Mas Amiel Maury; 1998 Quady Orange Muscat California Essence

## Chocolate Sorbet

1.1 L (1.2 quarts) cold water
100 g (³/₄ cup) cocoa powder
125 g (²/₃ cup) superfine sugar
65 ml (3¹/₄ tablespoons) glucose (or corn syrup)

Bring the water to a boil in a saucepan and slowly whisk in the cocoa powder until thoroughly dissolved.

Add the sugar and continue whisking until dissolved.

Bring the mixture slowly to a boil, then lower the heat and simmer for 10 minutes or until reduced by approximately a quarter.

Whisk in the glucose until it dissolves. Cover and refrigerate the mixture overnight or until completely chilled.

Churn the mixture in an icecream machine for 10–15 minutes, or according to the manufacturer's instructions.

**MAKES APPROXIMATELY 1 LITRE (2 PINTS)**

## Orange Ice Cream

*Orange paste comes in jars, and is available from specialty food stores.*

1 L (1 quart) fresh orange juice
10 egg yolks
100 g (½ cup) superfine sugar
zest of 1 orange
65 ml (3¼ tablespoons) glucose (or corn syrup)
3 teaspoons orange concentrate
300 ml (1¼ cups) whipping cream

Slowly bring the orange juice to a boil in a saucepan.

Gently whisk the egg yolks, then add the sugar and whisk together thoroughly.

Add the orange juice and zest to the egg mixture, and whisk together. Return the mixture to a low heat and stir with a wooden spoon for 5–6 minutes, or until it is slightly thickened and coats the back of the spoon.

Add the glucose to the mixture and stir until dissolved.

Remove from the heat and strain through a fine sieve, removing all zest and orange pith. Add the orange concentrate and stir thoroughly.

Set aside to cool, then cover and refrigerate for approximately 5 hours or overnight.

Add the cream to the mixture and churn in an ice cream machine according to the manufacturer's instructions.

**MAKES APPROXIMATELY 1 LITRE (2 PINTS)**

*Wine suggestions*
NV Chambers "Rosewood" Old Vines Muscadelle; 1998 Mas Amiel Maury;
1998 Quady Orange Muscat California Essence

# Basics

### Dashi

*Freeze-dried dashi is available or concentrated liquid is commercially available.*

1 L (2 pints) boiling water
2 x 10 cm (4 in) piece konbu
20–30 g (³/₄–1 oz) dried shaved bonito

Bring the water and konbu to a boil. When it begins to boil, take out the konbu and add the bonito. Turn off the heat and allow to sit for 1–2 minutes, then strain. For a stronger stock, increase the quantities of kelp and bonito.

**MAKES 1 L (2 PINTS)**

### Hijiki

Soak the hijiki in cold water for about 1–2 hours, then drain and place in a pot with equal quantities of sake, soy sauce, and mirin, and a pinch of sugar. If you need more liquid to cover, add more water, but take care not to add too much, since that will dilute the flavor of the hijiki. Cover and bring to a boil for about 10 minutes or so. Allow to sit until ready to use. Prepared hijiki keeps refrigerated for weeks.

### Ogonori

This comes fresh or salted in packets. Rinse thoroughly under running cold water, and taste. If it is too salty, soak for 10 minutes or so and rinse again.

### Scampi Oil

*I have made this with scampi, but it can be made with prawns, and is particularly good with seafood dishes.*

at least 12–15 scampi heads and shells
1 onion, finely chopped
1 stick celery, finely chopped
1 medium-sized carrot, finely chopped
1 clove garlic, finely chopped
6 sprigs thyme
300 ml (10 fl oz) water
4–5 tablespoons tomato paste
300 ml (10 fl oz) grapeseed or vegetable oil

Place all the shells in a small pot and crush with a hammer. Put a drop of grapeseed oil in a pan and sweat the shells over low heat until they are dry.

Add the onion, celery, carrot, garlic, and thyme, and sweat. Add the water, then the tomato paste. Be careful not to burn the ingredients, and to dissolve the tomato paste fully in the water. Add the oil, stir well, and bring to a boil. Then lower the heat and simmer for 1–1¼ hours. Take off the heat, and leave to sit for a while.

Strain, discarding the shells. Allow to stand: the oil and water should have separated. Skim off the oil and place it into a clean jar. Strain the remaining liquid through an oil or coffee filter and into a bowl. (The leftover liquid can be used as a soup or a sauce.)

**MAKES 300 ML (10 FL OZ)**

## Sugar Syrup

1 L (2 pints) water
500 g (1 lb) superfine sugar
200 g (6½ oz) glucose (or corn syrup)

Bring the water to a boil in a large saucepan. Slowly whisk in the sugar and glucose until completely dissolved. Bring the liquid back to a boil. Boil for 30 seconds to 1 minute only, then remove from the heat and allow to cool completely. Pour into an airtight container and refrigerate until completely chilled.

**MAKES 1 LITRE (2 PINTS)**

## Wakame

We use fresh wakame in the restaurant, which comes packed in salt. Put the wakame in a strainer and rinse, then cut into the size required. Run the wakame under hot tap water for a few seconds – the color will brighten. Rinse in cold water and squeeze dry.

Dried wakame is probably more readily available. To prepare, put the seaweed in a bowl of cold water and drain immediately. Allow to sit for 10–15 minutes. Feel the wakame: it should be soft. Do not soak in water or it will melt.

## Wasabi Mayonnaise

6 teaspoons wasabi powder
3 large egg yolks
½ teaspoon salt
1 tablespoon lemon juice
3 tablespoons rice wine vinegar
2 tablespoons soy sauce
2 tablespoons Dijon mustard
500 ml (16 fl oz) vegetable oil

Mix the wasabi powder with a little water to make a paste.

Process all the ingredients, except the oil, in a food processor. With the motor running, gradually add the oil in a steady stream until the mayonnaise reaches the desired consistency. You can add more wasabi to taste.

**MAKES ABOUT 500 ML (16 FL OZ)**

# Glossary

### ABALONE
A much prized delicacy. These molluscs are sold live, frozen, in cans, or dried. I use the fresh. They are available from good Asian food stores. Do not overcook the meat or it will toughen.

### AONORI
Green seaweed that has been flaked and dried, used to sprinkle on food after cooking. Sold in small glass shakers, and available from Japanese food stores. See also *seaweed*

### BLACK BEANS
Fermented soy beans. Most are sold in packets in Asian food stores. Check for saltiness, and adjust the seasoning.

### BLACK OLIVE PASTE
The Mediterranean paste of black olives, anchovies, capers, and olive oil, also known as tapenade. Taste for salt before using, and adjust the seasoning accordingly. You can make your own or purchase them ready-made from delicatessens and food shops.

### BLACK TRUFFLE PASTE
The paste of black truffles, available from good food shops.

### BONITO
Bonito is a member of the mackerel family, usually available dried but sometimes fresh. Thinly shaved dried bonito fillets, with *konbu*, are essential in the making of dashi (see page 169). Shaved dashi is sold in packets in Asian food stores, but choose one where the flakes look bright. Once the packet is open, store in an airtight container. Instant dashi (dashi-no-moto or hon-dashi) is now readily available in small glass jars or small sachets. Keep the jars tightly sealed.

### BUCKWHEAT
The dark grey, triangular seeds of the annual plant native to Central Asia. It is available from good food shops.

### BURDOCK
see *gobo*

### CHRYSANTHEMUM
Fresh, young leaves of the chrysanthemum plant can be used as a vegetable. Available from Asian produce markets.

### DAIKON
White radish, much used in Japanese and Chinese cooking. Available from Asian produce markets.

### DASHI
A Japanese stock made with *konbu* and *bonito* flakes. See the recipe on page 169.

### FIVE-SPICE POWDER
A traditional Chinese mixture of five spices: cinnamon, cloves, fennel seeds, Sichuan peppercorns, and star anise. Used in braises and stews. Readily available from all Asian food stores and supermarkets.

### GOBO
A root much used in Japanese cooking, usually about 1 m (slightly over 1 yard) long and 3 cm (1¼ in) thick. Scrub the skin well (do not peel) and keep immersed in cold acidulated water to remove bitterness and prevent discoloration. Used in braised dishes.

### GOOSE FAT
Available in small cans from good food shops and delicatessens.

### HIJIKI
see *seaweed*

### KELP
see *seaweed*

### KONBU
see *seaweed*

### LEMON-SCENTED OIL
A citrus oil available from good food stores and some delicatessens. Use sparingly.

### LEMONADE FRUIT
see *yuzu*

### MIRIN
The roe/eggs of the lobster.

**MIRIN**

A sweetened rice wine used for cooking.

**MISO**

The fermented paste of soy beans and usually rice or barley. There are many varieties. White miso is sweet and has a fine texture, which makes it ideal for soups and dressings.

**MIZUNA**

A mild mustard leaf used as a garnish or salad green.

**MORELS**

see *mushrooms*

**MUSHROOMS**

*Enoki* are mushrooms with thin yellow stems and tiny caps. They come in small clumps and are available fresh from Asian food stores. *Morels* have a globular or conical cap that has a honeycomb pattern. *Shiitake* mushrooms are dark brown with velvety caps. The dried and fresh are available in packets from Asian food stores and some produce markets now stock the fresh. *Shimeji* mushrooms have a distinctive dimple in their caps and a delicate flavor and texture.

**NORI**

see *seaweed*

**OGONORI**

see *seaweed*

**ORANGE OIL**

A citrus oil available from good food stores and some delicatessens. Use sparingly.

**PICKLED GINGER**

These are the pink pickled shoots of ginger, sold in Asian and Japanese food stores in jars.

**PLUM PASTE**

see *umeboshi*

**PRESERVED LEMON**

Lemons that have been preserved in salt and lemon juice, and sometimes, spices. To use, discard the pulp and finely chop the peel. Available from good food shops.

**SAKE**

Rice wine, which is used both as a beverage and cooking ingredient. Use in small quantities. It is available from liquor stores and Japanese food stores.

**SANSHO**

The seed pods of the Japanese prickly ash, which are ground and used as a spice. Available in small tins at Japanese food stores. Young sprigs of sansho (kinome) are also used as a herb or garnish.

**SEA CUCUMBER**

Usually available dried from Asian food stores.

**SEA URCHIN**

The dark yellow or orange roe is often eaten raw as sushi. Available from good fish suppliers.

**SEAWEED**

*Konbu* (kelp), with bonito, is one of the basic ingredients of dashi (see page 169). The dried leaves are sold in cellophane packets in Asian or Japanese food stores. *Tororo konbu* is seaweed that has been soaked in vinegar and shaved along the length of the leaf, then cut into threads. *Hijiki* is often sold dried, and is black and wiry. *Nori* is dried seaweed available in sheet form, commonly used to wrap sushi. It is sold in cellophane packets in most Asian food stores. Keep in an airtight container once the packet is opened. *Ogonori* is a very fine seaweed, often used as a garnish. *Wakame* is sold dried or fresh and salted. It is readily available from Asian or Japanese food stores. See page 169 for instructions on how to prepare hijiki and ogonori, and page 170 for wakame.

**SESAME SEEDS, BLACK**

These have an earthy taste compared to white sesame seeds. Available from Asian food stores.

**SHISO**

The leaf of the shiso plant (also known as perilla or beefsteak plant), used as a garnish and herb. Fresh mint can be substituted.

**SOBA**

Japanese buckwheat noodles, thin and brownish in color. Available in packets from Asian food stores and good supermarkets.

**SOY BEANS**

The beans from the soy bean pod, eaten as a fresh vegetable. The green beans are sold in packets in Asian food stores and are often frozen.

## SOY SAUCE

A salty sauce made from soy beans, wheat, and salt that is used as a seasoning.

## SUSHI RICE

Vinegared rice used for making sushi. Short-grain rice is cooked and a mixture of vinegar, sugar, and salt is stirred through the rice as it cools.

## SWEETBREADS

The thymus gland and the pancreas of calves and lambs. They need to be soaked in cold water for a few hours to remove any blood, then blanched in boiling water. Refresh in cold water, then proceed with the recipe.

## TONBURI

Also known as mountain caviar, this is a type of Japanese fern, used as a garnish.

## TORORO KONBU

see *seaweed*

## TRUFFLE

White and black truffles are much prized for their rich, earthy flavor. The fresh are sometimes available in Australia from specialist food stores and delicatessens. Canned and bottled varieties have little in common with the fresh, but are more readily available. When an ingredient (eg a peach) is "truffled," it has been infused with truffle oil.

## UMEBOSHI

Japanese pickled plums with a salty-sour flavor and a red color. These are available in packets from Asian food stores. Puréed umeboshi paste is available in small bottles or jars from Japanese food stores. The Chinese plum sauce is not a substitute.

## VINEGAR, BANYULS

A French-style vinegar, available from good food stores.

## VINEGAR, RICE WINE

A lighter and sweeter style of vinegar than western-style ones. Available in bottles from most Asian food stores and supermarkets.

## WAKAME

see *seaweed*

## WASABI POWDER

Horseradish, though unrelated to the western variety. The fresh root is sometimes available, but powdered or paste wasabi are readily available from Asian food stores. Powdered wasabi come in small round tins. Mix a little powder with water until smooth and allow to stand for the flavor to develop. Paste wasabi is ready to use.

## WHITE SESAME SEED PASTE

Not to be confused with tahini, sesame seed paste is made from toasted sesame seeds and is available in jars or cans from Asian food stores.

## WHITE TRUFFLE OIL

Available in small bottles from specialty food stores.

## WILD PEACHES

Available in jars from specialty food stores.

## YUZU

A Japanese citron. The zest has a bright, delicate citrus aroma and the juice is excellent in sashimi-style preparations. If yuzu juice is not available, use lemon juice instead, sweetened with a little sugar. *Yuzu kosho* is yuzu made into a paste with some chile. Yuzu is widely available in Japanese grocers.

## YUZU KOSHO

see *yuzu*

# Conversions

Metric units are used throughout this book. The approximate equivalents are as follows.

## DRY WEIGHTS

| | |
|---|---|
| 10 g | $\frac{1}{3}$ oz |
| 30 g | 1 oz |
| 50 g | $1\frac{3}{4}$ oz |
| 60 g | 2 oz |
| 85 g–90 g | 3 oz |
| 100 g | $3\frac{1}{2}$ oz |
| 125 g | 4 oz |
| 155 g | 5 oz |
| 185 g | 6 oz |
| 220 g | 7 oz |
| 250 g | 8 oz |
| 500 g | 16 oz (1 lb) |
| 1 kg | 2 lb |

## LIQUID WEIGHTS

| | | |
|---|---|---|
| 1 metric teaspoon | 5 ml | |
| 1 metric tablespoon | 20 ml | |
| 1 US teaspoon | 5 ml | |
| 1 US tablespoon | 15 ml | |
| $\frac{1}{4}$ metric cup | 62.5 ml | 2 fl oz |
| $\frac{1}{2}$ metric cup | 125 ml | 4 fl oz |
| 1 metric cup | 250 ml | 8 fl oz |
| 4 metric cups | l litre (2 pints) | $1\frac{3}{4}$ pints |

*Note: The US cup is slightly smaller than a metric cup.*

## OVEN TEMPERATURES

| | | | |
|---|---|---|---|
| 100°C | 210°F | Very slow | |
| 125°C | 240°F | Very slow | |
| 150°C | 300°F | Slow | Gas Mark 2 |
| 180°C | 350°F | Moderate | Gas Mark 4 |
| 200°C | 400°F | Moderately hot | Gas Mark 6 |
| 220°C | 450°F | Hot | Gas Mark 7 |
| 250°C | 475°F | Very hot | Gas Mark 9 |

# Index

# Suppliers

**BROWNE TRADING COMPANY**
*Fresh fish and shellfish*
260 Commercial Street
Portland, ME  04101
(207) 766-2402

**DEAN AND DELUCA**
*Truffle oils, vinegars, grains*
560 Broadway
New York, NY  10012
(800) 221-7714

**EUROPEAN IMPORTS**
*Foie gras, squab, truffles*
2745 North Elston
Chicago, IL  60647
(800) 323-3464

**GEO. CORNILLE & SONS PRODUCE**
*Fresh and specialty produce*
60 South Water Market
Chicago, IL  60608
(312) 226-1015

**MARINELLI SHELLFISH**
*Fresh seafood and shellfish*
Pier 33, Space P-22
The Embarcadero
San Francisco, CA  94111
(415) 391-0846

# Acknowledgments

I have been fortunate to have received help and learned from many people. I wish to acknowledge my admiration for the chefs and restaurateurs I have encountered along the way.

Thanks are also due to: Ferran Adrià, John Alexander, The James Beard Foundation, Gay Bilson, Tony Bilson, Daniel Buloud, Robert Carrier, Phillip Challis, Julia Child, David Dale, Michael Dowe, Jill Dupleix, Terry Durack, Sean Dwyer, Michael Gardner, Richard Geoffroy, Steven Greystone, James Halliday, Ray and Sean Harris, Huon Hooke, Lisa Hudson, Duilio Innocenti, Cynthia and Ted Jackson, Barbara Kafka, Thomas Keller, Shumei Kobayashi, Gilbert Lau, Lazaris family, Ottmar Liebert, Louise Lister, Carlier and Akio Makigawa, Yayoi Maloney, John Mangos, Lyndey Milan, Nobu Matsuhisa, Takashi Morieda, Drew Nieporent, Jacques Pepin, Armando Percuoco, Norman & Beppi Polese, Justin Quek, Gordon Ramsay, Rockliff family, Leo Schofield, Mitsuo and Christine Shoji, Mark Signorio, Colin Sim, Dr. Lee and May Smith, Kathy Snowball, Ronnie di Stasio, Gary Steele, Harvey Steiman, Robert Stevenson, Mr. and Mrs. Street, Robertson Swan family, Masa Takayama, Totsuka family, Charlie Trotter, Jean Georges Vongerichten, Anne Willan, Danny White, Norma Willis, Dr. Kwok Yan, and David Yem. Thank you all for your generosity. To the many more whose names do not appear here, my gratitude to you is as deep.

Without the support of loyal diners and friends of the restaurant, we would not be here today. Thank you all.

To all my suppliers, thank you for your attention to quality and excellence, for fulfilling my sometimes almost impossible demands and putting up with me over the years.

Special thanks must also go to my mother.

Thank you to my new friend Foong Ling Kong, for understanding my language and vision from the beginning, and giving me the words I needed to bring this book to fruition.

My sincere thanks to the original publisher of this book, HarperCollins, especially to Helen Littleton, commissioning editor, Katie Mitchell, designer, and Jane Morrow, editor.

To my longtime friend Jon Osbeiston from the Ultimo Wine Center, thank you for sharing the genius of your palate!

Finally, I wish to acknowledge my dedicated and talented team at Tetsuya's, who work very hard to make us all look good. To Judy Chandler, who has been with me since Ultimo's, thank you for your dedication and loyalty. To David Gumbleton, special thanks for giving up your vacations to help work on this book. My deepest thanks go to Vicki Wild for helping me remain focused and pushing me onwards. Without her encouragement and help, this book would not have been possible. I am humbled by your generosity.